ISBN 978-0-267-51090-0
PIBN 10291507

This book is a reproduction of an important historical work. Forgotten Books uses
state-of-the-art technology to digitally reconstruct the work, preserving the original format
whilst repairing imperfections present in the aged copy. In rare cases, an imperfection in
the original, such as a blemish or missing page, may be replicated in our edition. We do,
however, repair the vast majority of imperfections successfully; any imperfections that
remain are intentionally left to preserve the state of such historical works.

OF

YANKEE SULLIVAN,

EMBRACING FULL AND ACCURATE REPORTS

OF HIS

FIGHTS WITH

HAMMER LANE,

BOB CAUNT,

TOM SECOR,

TOM HYER,

HARRY BELL,

JOHN MORRISEY,

Together with a Synopsis of his Minor Battles from his first Appearance in the Prize Ring until his Retirement.

ALSO, THE BATTLES BETWEEN

TOM HYER AND COUNTRY M'CLEESTER,
CHRISS. LILLY AND TOM M'COY,
GEORGE KENSETT AND NED HAMMOND,
ALF. WALKER & JOE HOILES, the "Spider."

PHILADELPHIA:

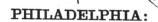

PREFACE.

IT is not actually necessary to write a preface to a work of this description; but, in offering to the public a collection of the various battles fought by Mr. SULLIVAN, we wish to add a few words in reference to the capabilities of one of the greatest pugilists of this or any other country. As a skillful boxer, as a hard-hitter, and as a tactician of the first order, Mr. Sullivan has no superior. He makes his calculations for a battle with a coolness and correct judgment seldom equaled, never surpassed; and the success invariably attending him in his contests is sufficient proof that his discrimination and keen perception have been carefully and systematically studied. No man was ever more safe to back than Sullivan, and those who ventured their money, did so with a perfect knowledge that, if they lost, it would not be for want of exertion in their man, for as long as there was the shadow of a chance left him, Sullivan would use his utmost endeavors to obtain the victory. In but one instance did he suffer defeat, and that was an honorable defeat—for, when we look at the great disparity in the size as well as the weight of the men, (Hyer and Sullivan,) it is really astonishing how he withstood the great odds against him as long and as courageously as he did, for the only clean knock-down blow in that great battle was given by Sullivan. It cannot be said of Sullivan that he ever "crossed" a battle, although he has had opportunities to do so, whereby he could have realised a handsome sum of money—he preferred to achieve a reputation for honest dealing in the prize ring, as well as for science and strength. He could always find backers to any amount, no matter who his competitor should be. In his battle with Morrissey, no one can deny that Sullivan was the victor, although the decision of the Referee lost him the money. That the decision was erroneous, according to the Rules of the Ring, admits of no question.

With these few remarks, we offer this work to the public, hoping it may meet with their approbation and encouragement.

THE EDITOR.

LIFE AND BATTLES

OF

YANKEE SULLIVAN.

"A COWARD—A man incapable either of defending or of revenging himself, evidently wants one of the most essential parts of the character of a man. He is as much mutilated and deformed in mind as another in his body, who is either deprived of some of its most essential members, or has lost the use of them."—*Wealth of Nations.*

In commencing our sketch of the Life and Battles in the Prize Ring, of Yankee Sullivan, as he is familiarly called, we do so, under the impression that it is called for at the present time by the sporting world, and by the fistic community more particularly, inasmuch as the late battle at Boston Corners, in which Sullivan was declared by the Referee to have lost the fight, finished his career in the Prize Ring, and enables us to give an outline of his first battles in England and Ireland, which were not considered of much importance at the period in which they were fought, as well as a full and detailed account of those Extraordinary Contests in England and in this country, which have rendered his name and abilities as a scientific pugilist familiar and famous throughout the entire sporting world.

James Sullivan, according to authentic information, was born on the 12th of April, 1813, at Banden, near Cork, Ireland, and is at this time nearly 41 years of age. During his boyish days he was always considered at the "head of the heap," having many a turn-up with his play-fellows, and generally came out of the muss "right side up with care." As he advanced in years, and began to develope more than common activity, strength and muscle, he was rather feared by his companions, who looked upon him as their leader ; and if any one of the "party" was not able to "stand his hand" against any of the members of other parties, Jim was always ready "to take it up," and soon finished the work cut out for him. It must not be supposed that young Sullivan always escaped punishment, or that he "came out as sound as he went in." In many instances he was severely bruised, but did not seem to care for hard knocks, and went in with a determination to "stand the storm, and win the fight."

His numerous successes, as a natural consequence, made him many enemies, and he was on several occasions way-laid by these enemies, and severely beaten. It was owing to one of these scrapes that he challenged to a ring fight a young fellow named Stewart. The latter, who was somewhat skilled in the use of his " bunch of fives," thinking he had an easy thing of it, as Sullivan had never before fought a regular prize fight, accepted Sullivan's challenge with the greatest readiness, and offered to make the stakes £12 a side. Some of the knowing ones of the vicinity in which Sullivan was brought up, having witnessed on different occasions the natural scientific abilities displayed by young Sullivan, and having also ascertained his powers of endurance, determined to back him against his more confident and practised adversary, and at the time appointed for depositing the stakes, Sullivan was *on* hand, with his money *in* hand ; and his opponent, as he saw Sullivan put up his stake, and covered it with his own, seemed to think, as he gazed upon the " pile," that it was " all his own." Sullivan, however, had his own suspicions about " that little pool," and intimated to his opponent that he " could have it as soon as he had won it !" However, matters were arranged for the contest, the seconds, referee, &c., appointed. The preliminaries being settled, each man went into training for a short time, and as the day appointed for the contest drew nigh, the excitement became greater. On the day of battle, quite an assemblage of the pugilistic fraternity were present, and betting was quite brisk, the odds being upon Stewart. Without going into further details of the battle, it is only necessary to say that Sullivan proved so quick in his movements, as to baffle the tremendous efforts made by his opponent to win the fight, and after a sharp contest of 2 hours and 20 minutes, Sullivan was declared the victor, and the stakes were given up to him on the succeeding day.

The success of Sullivan in this affair caused him to be looked upon with jealousy by several members of the profession, and it was not long before he was challenged by Dick Trainor, who was considered, at that time, and in that locality, a " hard knot," and a " tough one to tackle on to." The friends of Sullivan, elated with his success over Stewart, and fully impressed with the idea that he was bound to " make his mark in the world," were nothing lothe to take up the challenge, and on communicating with Sullivan in reference to the match, he instantly said he was ready to meet Trainor at any time he choose to designate. A meeting took place, and a match was made between Sullivan and Trainor, to fight for £50 a side. The first deposit of £10 a side was made, and at four subsequent meetings the balance of the £50 a side was deposited. As this was a good sum, and as both men were anxious to " finger the deposits," each one went into exercise, and under the assistance of their respective friends, with whom they had a " bout" occasionally, the time was looked forward to with anxiety by the " fistic community." The friends of Sullivan determined to give him a " good fitting out," and consequently were most assiduous in their attentions upon him. The day of battle arrived, and throngs of the " peasantry" wended their way to the battle ground. All things being in readiness, the " gladiators" entered the arena, and the fight began. Sullivan, cunningly, kept himself rather " quiet" during the first part of the battle, in order to draw his opponent, and by so doing, ascertain his peculiar mode of fighting, and so arrange his " little army of ten," as to " go in" at the proper moment, and endeavour to win. This course he pursued for a short time, his opponent getting in some stingers upon Sullivan, and thinking at the same time that as there was no fight in him, he would soon finish him. Sullivan, by this time, had " heard enough," and profiting by a knowledge of his opponent's tactics, though it cost him some bruises to gain that knowledge, he went to work. His well-directed blows so confused his adversary, and his scientific abilities were so unexpected to him, that he was almost panic struck, though he still fought on, and did his best to win the battle ; but after a hard fight of 1 hour and 45 minutes, during which time 73 rounds were fought, Trainor was unable to respond to the call of time, and Sullivan was declared the victor amid the plaudits of his friends. This victory proved him to be a man of strong natural scientific qualities, and his friends advised him to take proper precautions in regard to his future movements ; to engage in friendly set-to's whenever he had the opportunity, and that he would be able to " stand his hand" with the biggest of them. Sullivan followed this advice, sparred at benefits, took plenty of exercise, and tried to keep himself well up to the mark. He soon after engaged in a contest with George Sharpless, for £100 a side, and after fighting 1 hour and 5 minutes, Sharpless was defeated.

Having now gained for himself a name as a Ring Fighter, he kept aloof from the smaller fry, and determined, when the opportunity should offer, to have a "shy" at some of the "big ones." The opportunity was not long wanting,

for it happened that a dispute was going on at a public house in the neighborhood where Sullivan was residing, and a man named Tom Brady, a pugilist of the first class, thinking to take the " conceit out of Sullivan," as he said, entered into the discussion, and made such remarks of a personal character, as to touch a tender spot in Sullivan's feelings, and the latter rushed in to chastise his antagonist, but the friends of both interfered, and for the time stopped the fight. Sullivan however, sent a challenge to Brady, who at once accepted it, and the time was named for the battle. It was considered an unwise proceeding in Sullivan to match himself against a man of such acknowledged powers as Brady had previously proved himself to be, but Sullivan had no fears for the result, for he made up his mind that he would win the fight if he had a " fair shake," and his prophecy proved true enough, for after a fight of only 17 rounds, occupying but 30 minutes, Brady was done for, and Sullivan was awarded the battle.

Sullivan had now obtained a series of victories, and was looked upon as a tip-top man. Having nothing new on hand, he determined to visit America, and accordingly arrived here in 1838, stopping here about 12 months, during which time he had one or two " dashes," and having got a liking for the Yorkers, he determined to return home, and make arrangements for taking up his residence permanently in this country. On arriving in his native country, his friends, finding him rough and ready, with a tolerable knowledge of the art of self defence, determined to give him a chance in the London Prize Ring, and accordingly sent forth a challenge that he would fight any eleven stone man in England. This was a bold move on the pugilistic board, for at that time there were in England men of that weight in whose hands it was thought Sullivan would not have the shadow of a chance. However, the challenge appeared, and while some were wondering at the temerity of Sullivan, who had never before been heard of in the London Ring, the challenge attracted the attention of the friends of Hammer Lane, who at that time was looked upon as one of the best of his weight. Without more ado, Lane's friends, without his knowledge, accepted Sullivan's challenge, but on Lane's being made acquainted with the arrangement, he gratefully accepted the invitation of his London friends, more especially as it gave him an opportunity of regaining the confidence of his friends, which had been somewhat shaken by his battle with young Molineaux, in which the latter defeated him in 53 rounds, occupying 72 minutes. This battle was fought on the 9th of June, 1840. The challenge given by Sullivan having been accepted by Hammer Lane, we give the following authentic report of the fight, as taken from Bell's Life, of Feb. 7th, 1841.

It will be seen that Lane fought several rounds with his left hand only; his right hanging useless at his side. Although defeated, Lane lost none of that confidence which had heretofore been reposed in him.

GREAT FIGHT

BETWEEN

Yankee Sullivan and Hammer Lane,

FOR £50 A SIDE

February 2, 1841.

With the name of Hammer Lane, who is a star of the Birmingham school, our readers are acquainted. He is a hero, distinguished for the high charac-ter which he has maintained, and has been fairly rated as a bright sample of the school from which he sprung. As the successful opponent of Owen Swift, he was regarded as a man of no common talent; and, in fact, from his outset, his milling career has been distinguished by unbroken good fortune, until deprived of his well-earned laurels by young Molyneux. the black, in the month of June last, when, from an injury in his right hand, his chances of victory were extinguished. He had previously beaten Harry Ball, Hewson, Jack Green, Tass Parker (twice), Jack Adams, and Bing stokes, the Westminster Pet. His carriage is unquestionable, and his style of fighting scientific and effective, while his manners and general deportment are not only inoffensive but popular. He was born in 1815, and his fighting weight is 150 pounds, to which point he was brought on Tuesday last, being in perfect condition, and in all respects fitting for the scratch. He trained with Johnny Broome at Stockbridge, and it is needless to say, gained golden opinions by the steadiness and propriety of his conduct. With regard to Sullivan, he is unknown in the pugilistic circles; but he is stated to be a Yankee; but we are inclined to believe he is an Eastender; like Jim Ward, of Irish parents. By the articles, it was stipulated that his antagonist was not to exceed eleven stone, while he might catch weight. His age is 25, his height about 5 feet 10 inches, his frame muscular and well proportioned, his weight 11 stone 6 lbs., and his face, although he may deny his parentage, very like a Connemara ram, displaying all the fierceness and wildness of that war-like animal, barring the natural appendages in the shape of horns. As with Nick Ward, his induction to the mysteries of the English ring was intrusted to Peter Taylor, and he proved himself an accomplished pupil to a good master. On entering the ring he was accompanied by Peter Taylor and Harry Holt, and sported a green throttle-squeeze with yellow spots. Hammer Lane claimed the kindly offices of Johnny Broome and Fuller, and displayed a purple flag with yellow border. On stripping, both men showed their condition to be first rate. Lane displayed a playful, devil-may-care confidence, while Sullivan was as grave as a mustard pot, and looked as fierce as a devilled kidney. The odds at starting were 2 to 1 on Lane, which increased 5 to 4 and 3 to 1, the latter odds being taken to a large figure. At twenty-two minutes after four, operations commenced.

THE FIGHT.

Round 1st.—Sullivan was no sooner at the scratch, than he threw himself into a form which proved that there was nothing of the novice in his pretensions ; he led off vigorously with his left, which was prettily stopped, and he in turn stopped Lane's left and right. Good stops followed on both sides. Sullivan popped in his left, but did not get quite home, while Lane in the counter, caught him in the nob. " Kid him," cried some of Sullivan's friends, and he tried the feinting dodge, but Lane was not to be had. Sullivan waited steadily, his hands well up, when Lane broke ground and hit away left and right, a rally followed, in which there were some pretty exchanges without much advantage on either side, when Lane, from the state of the ground, slipped and fell. (Loud cheers for the Yankee.)

Round 2d.—Sullivan, of whose pretensions no mean opinion was formed, came up steady, and waited for the attack. Lane led off with his left, but was stopped. Some lively exchanges followed left and right, and after a short rally, Lane again slipped down laughing.

Round 3d.—Good counter hits with the left, one of which caught Lane on the mouth, and another dropped on Sullivan's ogle, which immediately showed a mouse. A lively rally close to the ropes, in which it was observed that Sullivan hit open handed. Lane closed and threw his man, with his head under his arm.

Round 4th.—On coming to the scratch, the dials of both were painted, and a tinge of blood was perceptible on Lane's lips from a touch on his ivories. Sulli-

van again stopped Lane's first effort with his left, and in return gave him another smack in the gob. Good stopping on both sides. Lane dropped his left on Sullivan's body. After an exchange of blows, Sullivan hit short with his left, and tried the upper cut, but missed. Lane in getting away slipped down, but rose laughing.

Round 5th.—Counter hit with the left and good exchanges left and right. A close, in which mutual fibbing took place, and Sullivan showed that he was quite awake to in, as well as out fighting. In the struggle for the fall, Lane got his man down.

Round 6th.—Lane came up laughing, hit out with his left, but was stopped ; he made a feint with his left, and succeeded in planting slightly with his right on Sullivan's pimple, which he followed up, after another cunning dodge, by a visitation from his left. Sullivan, nothing daunted, followed him up to the corner, caught his left hand with his right, and with his left gave him a whack in the chops. Lane broke away and commenced a fierce rally, hitting out left and right. Sullivan stopped both blows on the points of his elbows, and in an instant we observed, from the immediate swelling of his right fore arm, that Lane had sustained severe injury ; he, however, let go his left at the body, but dropping his right to his side, it was obvious that he had lost the power of using it. Still he jobbed with his left, which Sullivan rushed in and seized with his right, and in the close Lane fell, Sullivan upon him. (Although the injury to Lane's arm was only visible to us now, we learn that the mischief was done in the third round, and that the consequent use of the arm increased the fracture till further exertion became impossible. The bone called the *radius*, was completely fractured.)

Round 7th.—The extent of injury to Lane's right arm was not generally known, but on coming up it was seen that it was powerless ; in fact, he rested it on his body, and at once commenced fighting with his left. He jobbed Sullivan dreadfully on the snout, from whence he drew lots of claret ; he repeated the same dose in quick succession three or four times; from the rapidity, force, and straightness of the blows (Sullivan being unable to stop them), the hits were terrific, and severe cuts on the brow and cheek followed the previous visits on the nose, the Yankee exhibiting a woful spectacle, bleeding most profusely. Sullivan's friends now called loudly upon him to go in and fight, as Lane had but one arm. He responded to the advice, followed Lane as he retreated jobbing, to the corner. Sullivan attempted to close, but Lane slipped down. ˉ[It now became the question with Lane's backers from the state of his arm, whether prudence and humanity should not suggest the propriety of submitting to the consequences of this melancholy accident. Lane, however, resisted the suggestion, said he could lick him with one hand, and on time being called, came up to the scratch laughing.]

Round 8th.---Thrice did Sullivan, who confined himself to the defensive system, stop the hammerman's terrific left, whose right continued pinned to his side. Lane retreated to draw his man, jobbing him as he advanced. Sullivan hit short at the lame arm but missed, when Lane caught him heavily in the body with his left, and then, to the astonishment of the ring, repeated the like heavy blows with the same hand on the mouth and body with the rapidity of lightning, increasing the fractures in the Yankee's dial. Sullivan appeared quite bewildered, and hit short, but being called upon by his seconds and backers to go in, he followed their advice, but missed a right handed hit, and Lane went down laughing.

Round 9th.---Sullivan had now sufficient to do to stop the left handed hits of his gallant opponent, who, however, contrived to pepper him with unceasing vigor and effect, till, on Sullivan's boring in, he fell at the ropes to avoid a struggle.

Round 10th.---Lane again led off with his left, and retreated; Sullivan, amidst the bellowing of his friends, followed him to the corner, caught the offending weapon in his right hand, and was about to administer pepper with his left, when

Lane got down to avoid. [Sullivan's seconds claimed " foul," but the claim was instantly resisted as perfectly groundless.]

Round 11th.---Lane again gave his adversary [whose head exhibited a very lively representation of a " Field Lane duck, alias a b --y jemmy,"] a poke in the breadbasket and retired. Sullivan followed him at the score, and caught him with the right on the nob but open handed. Lane here retreated to the ropes but could not get farther, on which Sullivan seized him with both arms. Lane, perfectly powerless, could not get away; but in trying for the fall, instead of falling on him, Sullivan fell wide of his mark, and to the great amusement of the spectators.

Round 12th.---A strong feeling of sympathy for the fate of Lane now pervaded all quarters, but still he came up as game as a bull dog. Counter hits with the left. Lane endeavoring to follow up his favorite suit, hit short. In a second attempt he was more fortunate, and jobbed Sullivan dreadfully as he came in three times in succession, spinning the claret from his mug, like sparks from a pyrotechnic centre. Sullivan rushed in furiously, but Lane got down.

Round 13th.---Lane passed in a body blow with his left and retreated. Sullivan, who was nearly stunned by the repeated visitations to his pimple, rushed in and hit open handed with his left, and Lane got down.

Round 14th.---Lane pursued his jobbing system, hit between Sullivan's guard and muzzled him. Sullivan fought wild, and missed right and left, when Lane drew back, and met him as he came in, and gave him a tremendous smasher on the optic. Sullivan was " flabergasticated," when Lane dropped him a slashing hit on the nose.

Round 15th.---Sullivan came up a splendid object for a butcher's shop. Sullivan stopped Lane's left belt hit. Short in return. In the counter hits he was more successful, and being provided with a piece of oakum in his hand, he kept it closed. Counter with the left. Lane three times in succession passed in his favorite jobbers. Sullivan followed him up to the corner, when

Lane slipped under the ropes laughing, and exciting the admiration and wonder of the surrounding throng.

Round 16*th.*---Sullivan's left daylight all but extinguished. Lane passed in his left, but was short. Counter hitting with the left, in which Sullivan having contrived, by the advice of his seconds, to keep his short, caught Lane a tremendous whack on the left brow, cutting him severely, and dropping him close to the corner.

Round 17*th.*---Counter hits with the left. Lane passed in his left twice in succession on the head and body. He retreated, but on trying to repeat the dose, Sullivan stopped him, and was trying to return the compliment, when Lane slipped down to avoid. " Foul" was again claimed, which showed the desperate apprehensions entertained by Sullivan's seconds, but was again rejected by the referee.

Round 18*th.*---Still did Lane come up with unflinching courage, and delivered with his left on the head and body, retreating (cries to Sullivan, " go in and fight, he's got but one hand.") Sullivan obeyed the mandate, and caught Lane a heavy jobbing hit under the left eye. Lane down, bleeding.

Round 19*th, and last.*---Lane came up with less vigor than in former rounds, when Sullivan rushed in to fight, received a smack from the left, but returned with severity in the old spot, and Lane was again down. Sullivan, although dreadfully punished, being still strong on his legs.

Swift, and the backers of Lane, feeling that to protract the fight would be inhuman to Lane, gave in for him amidst loud cheers from the friends of the Yankee, who was proclaimed the victor, in 34 minutes.

REMARKS.

The extraordinary courage displayed by Lane on the occasion, fighting, as he did, thirteen rounds against a man of superior weight, excited the unmitigated admiration of all.

A more extraordinary display of British bravery never signalized the doings of the ring; and but for the judicious advice of Sullivan's friends, such was the extreme severity of the punishment administered, little doubt existed that he would have bitten the dust or rather snow, with which the battle field was covered. Had Lane commenced as he began in the 7th round, and contented himself with jobbing his man with the left as he came in, keeping his right in reserve, no doubt his labors would have quickly terminated. He seemed disposed, however, to try the metal of his opponent, and thus incurred an injury which, we consider, rendered his chance of success hopeless. Sullivan proved himself a greater adapt than was anticipated, and from the patience with which he sustained the severe punishment which he received, he is entitled to the character of a perfect " glutton :" and considering it was his first appearance in the English ring, he is entitled to every praise. Poor Lane was conveyed from the ground to a surgeon at Newbury, where the bone of his arm was secured by splints. The unfortunate fellow seemed to feel more for his backers than for himself. He was conveyed to town the next day, and showed at the " Bath," with his arm in a sling, and his left eye under a green *verandah.*

The result of the battle with Hammer Lane, while it gave great satisfaction to those who had sported their money on Sullivan, did not, however, gain him many friends, for it was the confident opinion of those well qualified to judge, that but for the accident by which Lane's arm had been rendered useless, Sullivan would have been defeated. This was merely opinion, however. Be this as it may, the friends of Lane were decidedly " down on Sullivan," and plainly made it manifest in more than one way, and on more than one occasion. The manner in which Sullivan endeavored to inflict additional punishment upon Lane's disabled arm was strongly commented on, and it was thought that some fresh disturbance might originate from the agitation of the subject, and, by

the advice of some friends, Sullivan determined to leave the country, and for this
purpose made all the arrangements necessary for his departure.   Early in the
spring of 1841, Sullivan bid adieu to the
land of his birth, to that green isle where
he had sported in boyhood's days, and to
part from which caused him many a bitter
pang.   After a long passage Sullivan
reached this city, and at once went to
work to look up some little habitation
where he might establish himself in business.   He was not long idle, having rent-
ed an old-fashioned house in Division
street, where he at once entered upon
the duties of publican, and as his battle
with Hammer Lane had rendered his name
familiar to the sporting world,' he soon
succeeded in drawing plenty of customers
to the "Sawdust House," as his tavern
was styled, and also in filling his till with
a plentiful sprinkling of the "almighty
dollar."   His house became the resort of
the pugilistic fraternity, and everything
seemed to work "fair and square." His
countrymen, who looked upon him as a
bright sample of the Emerald Isle, were
in extacies on account of his defeat of the
great Hammer Lane.   Some of the more
enthusiastic admirers of the "Yankee,"
as he was styled in England, after the battle with Lane, would get together of a
Saturday night, in a back room of the
Sawdust House, and over their well filled
glasses, would sing and talk of the exploits
of the daring Sullivan, who couldn't be beat.

It could not be expected where there
were such nightly assemblages of all classes
of sporting gentry, that unity and good-
will would be always predominant.   Many
little quarrels had already taken place,
though nothing of any great moment had
as yet startled the world from its usual
quiet.   However, a storm was brewing;
the friends of Sullivan, anxious to show

their readiness to back their gallant countryman, seemed more anxious to get up a
fight between Sullivan and somebody else,
they did'nt care who, than Sullivan did
himself, who quietly attended to the wants
of the "gentlemen at the bar," and by so
doing attended to the wants of the "gentleman behind the bar," for the silver rolled into his hands with the least trouble in
the world.   Probably Sullivan would have
preferred this mode of doing business, but
as his friends wished to "bring him out,"
and show the Yankees what the Irish lad
could do, he at last made a match with
an Englishman named Vince Hammond.

Hammond, we believe, resided at Philadelphia, and he having won the choice of
ground, selected a spot of ground on
League Island, about 10 miles south of
Philadelphia, on which to fight the battle.
The match was made for $100 a side. The
friends of each rallied for their particular
man, and betting was quite lively, a considerable sum of money being sported on
the "event."   Although Hammond had
his own ground to fight on, yet the backers and friends of Sullivan were "all alive,"
and on the morning of the 2nd of September, 1841, the lower part of Philadelphia
presented a bustling appearance, as different parties could be seen wending their
way to the scene of battle.   The ring had
been formed upon a level piece of ground,
and every thing promised fair for a "tip
top fight."   As the men entered the inner
ring, and stood eyeing each other like a
couple of "game cocks," it appeared a difficult matter to undertake to say. from appearances, how the contest would end.
Betting was about even, though the friends
of Hammond, in some instances, would
give odds for the purpose of getting a
bet.   There was much betting as to who
would succeed in bringing "first blood."
Sullivan had advised his friends to bet all   .

the money they could raise on his winning this point, and this coming to the ear of Hammond, he determined, if possible, to circumvent the wily Irishman, and gain the advantage himself. Thus the bets offered by Sullivan's friends on first blood, were cheerfully taken up by his opponents.

Thus matters stood when the men walked to the scratch at the call of time, and began

THE FIGHT.

Sullivan had been well taken care of and looked for all the world as if he had been purposely cut out for a fighting man. Hammond was not exactly in as good trim as his friends desired he should be, nevertheless it was thought he would be able to give a good account of himself. On the men getting to the scratch, Hammond immediately went to work, and sent in his right, which reached the Yankee's upper lip, the blow just being hard enough to cut the inner skin, and send the blood trickling down his teeth. Having the interest of his backers at heart, and wishing to save them the large sums bet on his winning "first blood," he instantly clenched tight his lips and drew the blood in ere it was perceived by the friends of his opponent. Then with the rapidity of lightning, he let fly at Hammond, catching him a tremendous cut, splitting open his cheek, and drawing an abundance of the ruby liquid. The strength of the blow sent Hammond reeling, and as he staggered back, Sullivan, clapping his hands in delight, cried out "first blood," and then retired to his corner in the best of humor. It is enough to say that Sullivan, after the first round, had the fight all his own way, as he was enabled to hit Hammond as he pleased, without receiving the least punishment in return. Hammond's face was literally cut in gashes, the blood running from the wounds in all directions, and dying not only his own, but also the body of Sullivan. Hammond was nothing in the hands of Sullivan, as after fighting but eight rounds, occupying only ten minutes, Sullivan was declared the victor. Sullivan proved himself a clever tactician in this battle, and also gave evidence that he was not wanting in cunning, as the little incident narrated above testified.

The defeat of Hammond caused a great glorification among the friends of Yankee; and Country McCleester, a firm friend of Sullivan, wishing to have a "finger in the pie," caught a fight with Hyer, in which he, McCleester, was defeated. This rather elated the American portion of the pugilistic fraternity, and as Hyer was thought to be the one most likely to take down Sullivan, a match was talked of by the two. As Hyer would fight for nothing less than $3000 aside, Sullivan's friends were obliged to "drop the subject," inasmuch as this sum was rather beyond their means. However, willing that Sullivan should have another dash in the magic circle, a man named Secor was produced by the opponents of Sullivan, and though a formidable looking man, Sullivan accepted the banter, and a match was made for Secor and Sullivan to fight, on the 22d of January, 1842. Thus the two factions were satisfied for the time, and betting commenced on the result in good earnest. Secor being a heavy man, it was thought that Sullivan would meet with a defeat, but he had his own thoughts on the subject, and went into active training for the fight. The following full and authentic report of the battle is taken from the Sporting Chronicle of that date :

GREAT FIGHT
BETWEEN YANKEE SULLIVAN
AND THOMAS SECOR,
ON SATURDAY JANUARY, 24 1842,
AT STATEN ISLAND.

We rose at an early hour on Saturday morning to embark to see the long talked of fight between the renowned Yankee Sullivan and Thomas Secor. On sallying forth, we found the sky slightly flecked here and there with light feathery clouds, and a soft south-westerly breeze breathing a moderate and bracing freshness through the atmosphere.

At half-past 8 o'clock we started in the Boston, steamer, preceded by the Citizen (Secor's boat), the Star (Sullivan's boat), and the steamer Dream, and were followed by the steamer Wave. Thousands who were disappointed in getting aboard, lined the wharves and ran in crowds up and down the river side. The order of the day was, that all the boats should follow Sullivan's, who was to select the ground. There appeared, however, to be some indecision in regard to the matter, for after arriving opposite the heights of eternal Neversink, the champion's boat backed irresolutely to and fro for some time, and kept the others playing about like attendant dolphins. At length it was resolved to land at a wharf on Staten Island about 1-2 a mile north of old Fort Tompkins, and at a 1 4 to 11 A. M. the whole party disembarked. The singular multitude streamed in one long unbroken line along the heights towards the south, some bearing huge stakes, others ropes, and two or three a pickaxe, terrifying the simple inhabitants of the neighborhood with the savage irruption, and spreading even an uncertain alarm among the blue coated U. S. gentry from the fort, who came running in crowds to look on the strange array.

The spot pitched upon was upon the beautiful grounds of Mr. Aspinwall, of this city, within a few hundred yards of the light house at the " Narrows," and about half a mile from Fort Tompkins. There were about 2,000 spectators of all classes and descriptions on the ground. At 3-4 to 12 the stakes were driven and two rings formed, the inner one twenty-four feet square for the combatants and their seconds, and the outer one, very large, so as to afford a convenient circle for the large number on the ground. The spot was peculiarly adapted to the business in hand, as it lay at the foot of an abrupt slope of two or three hundred yards, which afforded a capital stand for the lookers on, and the close shaven sod was rendered soft and elastic by the action of a bright and beautiful sun.

While the preparations were going on, Sullivan walked about among the crowd, surveyed the arrangements with a cheerful and accustomed eye, and bantered several of his opponents with a bet of fifty to thirty-five dollars upon himself. At twenty minutes to 12, every thing being ready, the men commenced to peel. Five minutes afterward they entered the Ring, and confronted each other, stripped to the buff above the middle, while their nether array consisted of the professional corduroys and hose. Sullivan was the first to enter, his tile had been previously cast in by his second McClusky, and Secor's hat followed by the hands of Vanderzee. Previous to confronting each other, Sullivan nailed his color—a shred of black muslin—to one of the stakes, and Vanderzee addressing himself to the assemblage remarked, that his principal wanted nothing but " a fair and honest thing."

THE MEN.

When the men confronted each other, the superiority of Secor's size was very apparent, though to practised eyes he was plainly too fine. His flesh had a healthful ruddy glow, and the only fault of his condition was that there was a little too much of it. Of his physical proportions, we have spoken elsewhere, so need not recapitulate them in detail. We have but to repeat that he is defective in the chest, which is rather flat, and his shoulders incline to be round. In short, he is by no means such a man as we should select as calculated to become celebrated in the prize ring, though sooth to say he is a man of great physical strength, strength however which is encumbered and embarrassed by other points that form no part of the neceesary *tout ensemble* of a gladiator.

Sullivan, on the other hand, with a single physical exception, may be said to be the very model of a man of his weight and size. In height he is 5 feet 10 inches, his frame is round, his limbs muscular and clean with the exception of a slight inflection of his knees. His head is small and round, and has the appearance of being bone, features and all, from the boldness of its angles, the remarkable closeness of the skin, and the apparent impenetrability of its texture. His flesh was clear, what he had of it, and clung with peculiar tenacity to his body. We do not know his exact weight, but believe the difference between him and his antagonist to be about 23lbs.

THE FIGHT.

Round 1st.—At 15 minutes to 12, after the principals and seconds had shaken hands, all together, across each other's arms, the two combatants came merrily up to the scratch. Sullivan gathered himself up in his peculiar style, like a tiger preparing himself for a spring, and Secor brandished his arms warily up and down, while he at the same time eyed his antagonist with an intense and determined gaze. Secor led off with his right, which was followed by Sullivan as quick as lightning upon his antagonist's nose ; Sullivan then went to the ground to avoid the return. (Cries of "First blood for Sullivan!" and "he went down without a blow!")

Round 2d.—Both right to work. Sully stopped, and returned a slinging smack on the nose, starting the blood again ; answered by Secor with a Paixhan shot on, the nob, which knocked Sullivan out stiff and he fell clear to the ground on his back. When he was carried to his corner by his seconds, he pointed tauntingly at Secor's nose, and made faces at him.

Round 3d.—At it sharp again. Sullivan led off upon the mouth, cutting it again, and as Secor followed up, he planted, in his retreat, two more in the same place and then went down to avoid the return, laughing from the ground in Secor's face, who unwillingly had to turn away without touching him on the ground. This system of mocking and pointing the finger at his antagonist was pursued by Sullivan from the start, for the purpose of exasperating him and throwing him off his guard, and was in a slight measure successful. We cannot suppose it prac-

tised for any other purpose, as Secor was by no means an enemy to excite any man's contempt.

Round 4th.—Yankee led off again upon his old spot, on the nose, as true as a trivet and sharp as a knife, following it up, in his retreat ; then seeing trouble coming, he slipped away from it like a shadow and laughed in his baffled opponent's face.

Round 5th.—Both came up briskly; Secor made a feint and Sullivan went to the ground without a blow. (Murmurs of dissatisfaction from Secor's friends and a laugh from Sullivan.)

Round 6th.—Sullivan commenced in good earnest, planted three successive blows in Secor's face, one on either eye, and one on the old spot, starting the claret again in streams; he then dropped away from the return, and went to his corner laughing contemptuously again.

Round 7th.—Secor caught it again on the mug, and ere he could reply, Sullivan took to the ground.

Round 8th.—Secor came up fierce and went right to work. He let fly with his left, caught Yankee on his collar bone, turned him half way round, and followed with his right on the shoulder blade with such force as to cause an abrasion of the skin and make a noise resembling a pistol crack. Sully returned, but did not get home, and Secor caught him on the frontal bone and sent him to the ground.

Round 9th.—Yankee stopped, let fly with his left, caught Secor on the nose in the old place, and went down laughing to avoid the return.

Round 10th.—Sullivan bled his man this time the same way, and went down laughing again.

Round 11th.—Secor led off, was stopped, caught a return blow on his gory nose that sent the claret flying in a spray and widened the cleft already made. Secor rushed in, closed and threw his man, falling on him. Sullivan went to his corner laughing at him.

Round 12th.—Sullivan led off in earnest, planting blow after blow in his opponent's face. Secor, made wild by his punishment, returned at random, and Sullivan went down laughing.

Round 13th.—A rally and Secor nearly thrown over the ropes.

Round 14th—A rally, a close and Sully down.

Round 15th.—Sharp counter hits, a rally, Sullivan driven to the ropes and half pressed through them by Secor, who fell upon him. Sully returned to his corner laughing as before.

Round 16th.—Sullivan sent the claret from Secor's nose into fine spray again by a stinging smack ; Secor rushed in and closed, but Sullivan turned him and Secor went to the ground.

Round 17th.—Smart exchanges, a close, a rally and both down.

Round 18th.—Secor hit out right and left, a rally, Sully driven to the ropes, a clinch, a short struggle, ineffective ex changes and Sullivan nearly pressed through the ropes.

Round 19th.—A sharp rally, a close and both down.

Round 20th.—Both commenced earnestly ; counter hits, a rally, a close and Sullivan pressed to the ropes, when Secor fell over him bodily.

Round 21st.—A rally, Secor caught it sharply on his snuff box again, painting the fist of his antagonist ; close and Sullivan went down leaving Secor dreadfully jobbed.

Round 22d.—Sullivan let fly with his left three times with terrific effect, completely distracting his enemy, who rushed at him with open hands and arms ; Sullivan admonished him once more of his carelessness by a sharp cutting blow, and went to the ground laughing at him.

Round 23d.—Secor a little shy, let fly with his right, was stopped and caught it in return on his snuff taker, the blood jetting out into spray from the force of the blow, in all directions ; Secor rushed in, clinched and pressed his man to the ropes and fell on him.

Round 24th.—Secor's eyes were now both cushioned and variegated with their frequent visitations ; his face was covered all over with the blood which at the end of every round streamed profusely from his nose. He came up this time with a stupid and dogged determination ; led off, struck short and wild, caught an admonisher in the old place in consequence, and Yankee went down out of the way of an ugly blow.

It was now apparent to every body that Secor with his bold, straight forward mode of fighting, could not contend successfully with his wily and active adversary. Blow after blow came raining in upon him, drawing blood at every visitation, and when he would have returned the compliment, his antagonist slipped away from him like a shadow, and his blow, wasted in the air, had no other effect than that of straining him and pitching him forward over his tormentor Sullivan went down.

Round 25th.—Secor came up groggy ; both his eyes were half shut, and the blood clotted his nose and chin, and covered his face. He went in with good will, was punished in the old place and Sullivan went down.

Round 26th.—Secor went in wild, with open arms and hands, struck out and fell without a blow. (Cries of "he's gone ! The fight is over ! &c.")

Round 27th.—Sullivan merry, smart counter hits, a close and Sullivan was thrown, Secor falling heavily on him.

Round 28th.—Secor went in well, got a heavy blow and closed, Sullivan whirled him round and threw him.

Round 29th.—Secor much fatigued and Sullivan fresh, fierce exchanges, a rally and Secor carried Sullivan half over the ropes, falling on him and trying by his weight to force him outside.

Round 30th.—Sullivan jobbed his man dreadfully, Secor returned wildly. Notwithstanding his severe punishment, he followed his tormentor all round the ring, smiling at him through his blood. A rally and Sullivan thrown half over the ropes on his back, Secor on top of him jobbing him in the face.

Round 31st.—Smart exchanges, Secor wild and streaming with blood ; he rallied, drove Sullivan to the ropes, who dropped away from a heavy blow and laughed in his face ; Secor's eyes nearly closed.

Round 32d.—Sullivan got in two in his old place, a close and Secor fell heavily upon him.

Round 33d.—Secor caught it again and Sullivan dropped.

Round 34th.—Another stinging smack on Secor's nose ; Sullivan dropped, and Secor in bitter disappointment stood stupidly gazing at him.

Round 35th.—After receiving two severe cuts in the face, Secor rallied, pressed Sullivan to the ropes, where a clinch took place and Secor lifted him half over;

they then mutually jobbed each other very severely for some minutes, during which, amid cries of " Secor's got him at last, give it to him Secor! &c." the ring was broken in. After order was restored, the two combatants went at it again with renewed vigor and determination. From this to the fiftieth round, followed a succession of rounds, during which Secor came up with a dogged obstinacy, received two or three terrific cuts in the face, jollowed, closed and pressed his man to the ropes, falling in one or two instances, heavily upon him.

Round 51st.—A rally, a close, Secor broke away and gave the upper cut, another close and Sullivan down.

Round 52d.—Wild exchanges, Secor stopped, let fly with his right, caught Sullivan on the ear and struck him down

Round 53d.—After throwing in two stingers on the nob and nose, Sullivan went down.

Round 54th.—Secor caught a severe body blow, returned it lightly and Yankee went down.

Ronud 55th.—A close and Sullivan down.

Round 56th.—Secor more and more hopeless, a close and Sullivan down.

Round 57th.—Secor very groggy, struck wild, and caught it very bad in return, Sullivan down at the ropes.

Round 58th.—Secor freshening a little, Sullivan down at the ropes.

Round 59ty.—Secor, though stupid and groggy with punishment, came up well, caught a severe neck blow, followed by another on the chin, mutual hits and both, down.

Round 60th.—Sharp counters, both down, Sullivan under.

Rovnd 61st.—Secor coming up slow but willingly. A rally, and Secor down at the ropes.

Round 62nd.—Secor caught it again on the nob, rallied and carried his man down at the ropes.

Round 63rd.—Secor failing fast, got jobbed badly right and left, and went down hopelessly with the upper cut.

Rouna 64th.—Sharp work, Secor suffering, went down with a tremendous body blow.

Round 65th.—Secor was now hopelessly weak; with good heart, however, he staggered up to his man and received his punishment with dogged game. More than this cannot be said. It was mere cruelty to suffer him to go in any more, and he was only allowed to do so at his own urgent entreaties. In this round he came up readily and free, but after a blow in the face, Sullivan put down his arms as if dealing with a child. Another blow carried him down.

Sullivan now came forward, and offering his hand to Secor, advised that he should be withdrawn as it was now absolute butchery to strike him. Secor took his hands but refused his advice.

Round 66th.—Sullivan got in three severe cuts and Secor fell heavily to the ground.

Round 67th.—Time was called. Secor was ready, but his seconds refused to allow him to enter. He begged for a few more trials, but at length suffered himself to be refused. Sullivan was declared the victor amid the acclamations of his friends. All hands then pulled up stakes and made tracks for the boats.

This fight bears its own comment. The whole description may be summed up, by saying that Secor stood up and took his whipping like a man. With his inadequate science and superior size, he looked like a giant suffering the inflictions of some malicious spirit, impalpable to his attacks. The mode of fighting adopted by Sullivan has been much descanted on in England and lately here. It is in just disrepute, and though not ruled "foul" by regulations of the prize ring, it is not considered "fair" by any of the Fancy. The practice was introduced by the Wards in England, and practised particularly by Nick of that name. Caunt had to endure it in his fights with the latter, and Brassey was beaten by Tass Parker, a much lighter man, last summer, in the same way. The reporter of that contest speaks with great indignation of the "dropping system," and denounces it as unfair under any circumstances. We cannot say that we think Sullivan has gained any credit in this achievement. We always thought hom a first rate man of his weight, and our opinion is still the same.

Sullivan was seconded by Coutry Mc. Clusky and William Ford.

Secor, by A. Vanderzee and F. Speights.

The former left the ground quite fresh, while his antagonist was in a most pitiable situation. Most of his injuries, however, are in his face, which is dreadfully swollen, and his nose is literally split in two.

Sullivan, though he displayed no hurts of consequence in the face, yet received some severe injuries on his body, from the effects of which he must suffer not a little. Time—One hour and five minutes.

The result of the last mentioned fight, wherein Sullivan defeated a man who was much superior to him in size and strength, gave renewed encouragement to the friends of the Yankee, who were in raptures with the fighting abilities so bravely displayed by the cunning Yankee. The ruse adopted by him to save for his backers and friends the money sported on the event of " first blood " was looked upon as a " capital good thing," and so it was, though how far it was in accordance with honest and correct principles, we are not bound to say, though it has doubtless served as an example to subsequent competitors of the wily Irishman, to keep a bright look out upon the manœuvres of the cunning boxer. The manner in which Secor stood the whipping, reflected great credit upon him as a man of true courage, and had he been possessed of a tithe of the scientific abilities displayed by his opponent, he must, in all probability, have won the fight. The " dropping system," adopted by Sullivan, was not looked upon as the " fair thing " for a fair and scientific pugilist to indulge in, and his friends would have preferred to have seen him win the fight in a straightforward and manly way ; but others again stated that the disparity in the size of the two combatants fully compensated for any little advantage taken by Sullivan, he being the smaller man.

The fighting spirit was now in the ascendency, and as the friends of Secor were determined to " take down " the Irishman, they cast their eyes round about the pugilistic circle to find a man capable of holding up the honor of the Stars and Stripes against the encroachments of the Green Flag of the Emerald Isle. The science of pugilism having been indulged in but to a limited degree in America, a " good man " could not be " picked up " at a moment's warning, and it was promised that when the proper man should be found, the Yankee would be on hand to meet him. In the mean time a couple of descendants of the " peculiar institution of the South," met at Hoboken, on the 1st of June, 1842, and fought for $25 aside. The names of the " culled gemmen " were Dan Knox and Sam Briggs. After fighting 7 rounds in 18 minutes, Knox sent in so many *knocks* as to knock his opponent out of time. The week ensuing, a fight took place at Hoboken between two pugilistic aspirants, named Sandy Stewart and Jim Williams. They fought for $50 aside, and after a contest of 11 minutes, fighting in that time 8 rounds, Stewart was the winner. Numerous fights, of more or less importance, were continually taking place about this time, all owing no doubt to the state of feeling existing in relation to the Stars and Stripes versus the Green Flag.

Six months had now elapsed since the battle between Sullivan and Secor, and yet no one had been brought forward since that event to test the title to superiority. Sullivan was in his prime, and his praises were sung by his enthusiastic countrymen. In fact, the Yankee was looked upon as " cock of the walk.

The boys were around, however, and as the sporters of New York City had not been able thus far to put Sullivan out of conceit of himself, the " ever-ready lads of Brooklyn " looked throughout the " City of Churches " for a man " suited to their mind."

It happened about this period that a man named Bell, who had been teaching the good people of Brooklyn how to defend themselvs against the "wily influence of foreign encroachments," by *force of arms*, and who was looked upon as a most skilful exponent of the science of the magic circle, attracted the attention of the knowing ones of Brooklyn as being the very man they had been so long looking for. Bell was sorry he had not been discovered sooner, but really if these gentlemen had merely intimated that he, Bell, was wanting, he would have cheerfully responded to the call. A few moments conversation soon explained matters, and a mutual understanding was soon arrived at between the " professor and his pupil." Thus, by his ready acquiesence in the wishes of the pugilistic fraternity, Bell proved that he was by no means a *dumb-bell.* Sullivan and his backers were soon made acquainted with the state of affairs, and as the Yankee wanted to keep his " hand in," he agreed to meet the friends of the opposite party to make arrangements for " *striking the Bell,*" although he preferred " ringing in " the change at his place of business, where he could " give and take " with the greatest good will in the world, and never " went down to avoid a return."

A short time after the fact had been made known to Sullivan that his "bunch of fives" were to be called into play again, the friends of both men met, and agreed that a " Prize Fight for $300 a side should take place between Sullivan and Bell, on Monday, 29th of August, 1842." After the announcement had been publicly made that the heretofore victorious Irishman was matched for another set-to, the excitement became greater than ever, and it was confidently expected from the well known attainments of Bell in " the art and mysteries of shoulder hitting," although we believe he had never before engaged in a prize fight, that he would be fully able to vanquish his cunning adversary, and uphold the honor of "the city of churches." Notwithstanding the formidable appearance of things, Sullivan and his friends were by no means discouraged, but at once made preparations for the day of trial. In Brooklyn, the " boys' were " all alive," and in some cases " kicking," for many a knock-down argument was had upon the merits of the respective men. Although Sullivan had a numerous circle of friends in the religious city, still it was apparent that Bell was the favorite with the masses, inasmuch as he " was one of them."

The following description of the battle, and incidents connected therewith, is taken from the " Spirit of the Times," of September 3, 1842.

FIGHT
BETWEEN
SULLIVAN AND BELL,
FOR $300 A SIDE,
At Hart's Island, near New York,
ON MONDAY, 29th AUGUST, 1842.

This long expected " mill" came off on Monday last. As a precaution against magisterial interference, the precise field of encounter was not definitely known, except to those immediately concerned, (though it was generally understood that Hart's Island was to be the locale,) and such of the Fancy as wished to be spectators, were merely directed to embark at certain points and follow the combatants' boats. Though the previous evening had threatened unfavorable weather, the sun rose unobscured and warm, and as early as seven in the morning, the river swarmed with heterogenous thousands, waiting for their respective "locomotives," canvassing meanwhile, the merits of either combatant, and speculating upon the results of the day.

At 9 o'clock all were afloat, and the Westchester, [Sullivan's boat,] Napoleon [Bell's] Saratoga, Superior, Wave, Williamsburgh, Boston, Wm. Youngs, and Jacob Bell, with their heaped up masses, rocking to and fro in the stream, looked like some infernal cortege seeking the waters of the Styx, or a savage eruption bursting forth for ravage and for plunder.

Sullivan, who from the "toss', had the right of selection, chose Hart's Island, [about 20 miles from New York city,] and at half past ten the whole flotilla lay abreast of it. 'Here a serious difficulty presented itself in the fact that there was no dock or other landing place, and the long, shallow shelving shore made it dangerous for the heavily laden vessels to approach too near. The only mode of reaching land was by the medium of small boats, but many of the ardent amphibii, unable to wait their tedious turn, plunged headlong into the water and swam to shore. Thus gradually disembarked, the party streamed in one dense line in a N. E. course across the Island, and resembled, as they picked their devious way along, the writhings of a monstrous snake.

The spot appeared to us peculiarly unfit to the business on hand. There was no available landing place; the whole surface of the island is covered with a long, rank grass and stunted thorny shrubbery, growing in a soil of loose shifting sand. Even the field of fight, a natural arena comprising the only available spot on its surface, was of a comparatively circumscribed size, and though covered with a firmer soil, was "lumpy" and uneven. Worse than all, the ring, instead of being surrounded by a natural acclivity for the advantage of spectators, stands in the centre of an almost even plain, and thus robbed four fifths of the horde of even so much as a glimpse of the contest. These disadvantages were at once apparent, and from the moment of arrival there commenced " a scene of rude commotion " and ferocious struggle for the ring. Four times was a large outer circle made, and as often did the wild and insane savages break it in. For ourselves, in the first struggle, we were fortunate enough to obtain a hold of the rope ; and concluding by this that we were in a streak of luck, determined to " *rush it*," and in each succeeding struggle were equally successful. At last, with our knees forced devotionally two or three inches in the soil, our shoulders bearing the weight and press of three or four sweaty proximitants, with the sun pouring down his fiercest vertical rays upon our uncovered caput, and boiling the effluvia thrown off from the neighboring bodies into a floating lava of most execrable odor, we saw the gladiators enter the ring.

THE MEN.

At half-past one the men confronted each other. Sullivan looked in prime condition. His flesh was clear, his manner gay, and his air confident. He was the picture of a pugilist—small gladiatorial head—quick, bright eye—dial, which from the boldness of its angles and the tightness of its flesh appeared to be a mask of bone—round—deep in the chest—clean limbed, and possessed altogether of a frame which gives remarkable indications of activity and strength.

Bell did not wear the same appearance of gaiety and confidence. He entered the ring with a half careless, half reluctant swagger, which showed that he was not perfectly at ease, and to our mind, his cap did not follow his opponents quick enough in answer to the customary challenge. He is taller than Sullivan by an inch and a half, but not so faultlessly cut out. His chest is not so well developed or head so well set, and though carrying ten pound more weight we should call Sullivan (in a pugilistic sense) the heaviest man, for he has that weight in his fighting points which Bell has in his long slender legs. A singular indication was given, in shaking hands, of the difference of breeding and manners between certain classes of English and American society. Sullivan took his opponent's hand and gave a short, careless jerk of his nob at him—he was but the prize fighter—while Bell, who has been Americanized by his long residence among us, gracefully bent his head, and gave a courtly smile—he would be thought a gentleman.

THE FIGHT.

Bell won the flip for the choice of position and stationed himself on the lower side of the ring with the sun on his back. He was attended by KENSETT, of Baltimore, and McGEE. Sullivan was waited upon by his old assistants, FORD and COUNTRY McCLEESTER. Both were dressed in light net breeches and stockings, and blue belts spotted with white.

Round 1st.—Time was called and both came cheerfully up to the scratch.--- They shook hands again slightly, Bell very cautiously, as if fearful of a rough return for his politeness, and then squared for the combat. The rude murmurs of the turbulent multitude were at once hushed as death. Not a breath was heard. Scarcely a leaf was seen to stir. The primeval silence of that solitary spot was never more profound. In the centre of that vast arena stood the combatants—two bold men—confronting each other in full position, with momentary awe, and gathering their energies for the terrific struggle. Directly behind, stood the seconds of each, their forms slightly bent, their arms unconsciously outstretched and watching every movement of the principals with a feverish anxiety. The whole formed such a picture as one may seldom see. At length Sullivan broke the spell and imperceptibly advanced. He is an old general and knows the advantage of fighting in the enemy's country. Bell cautiously retreated and in answer to a feint showed his wariness by a start as rapid as electricity. At length Sullivan edged him out of his advantage of the sun, and getting it full in Bell's eyes, let drive a straight forward blow, which took effect under the left ogle.

Bell countered at the same time and caught his opponent on the cheek bone ; then followed two or three rapid exchanges, after which Bell rushed in, and at the end of a short struggle, Sullivan threw him handsomely and fell on him.

"Then rung from earth to sky one wild hurrah !" mingled with clapping of hands and various other expressions of wild applause. Bell rose smilingly and went to his corner, with a slight discoloration under the eye, upon which some of Sully's friends shrieked out a claim to the "first blood."

Round 2d.—Both came merrily up, their glossy skins unsullied by the previous scuffle. Yankee, who had now felt his man, determined on sharp fighting. He went right to work, got a sharp body blow and stopped a wicked return. Bell rallied, closed and pressed him to the ropes ; then ensued a short violent struggle, which ended in both flying through the ropes and falling hard, nearly side by side. Bell rose and returned to the ring, while Sullivan lay with his eyes closed and apparently insensible. He was lifted and carried to his corner with his head drooping languidly and even while undergoing sponging, &c., betrayed no sign of consciousness—a deep finesse. Many who did not know where to have him, cried out. " Ah, ha ! he'll never come to time !"

Round 3d.—When " time" was called Sullivan slowly rose and walked heavily to the mark ; but when there and confronted with his enemy, as quick as lightning, he "cast his nighted color off" and stood the very incarnation of the spirit of mischief. He led off amid cries of "Ony luk at the divil !" from some admiring Patlanders.

Round 4th. Billy opened the ball with a well-meant right-hander, but was stopped, and stopped one himself in return. He then got in a heavy body blow, which carried his man away three or four feet. Sully came back, wickedly pursing his mouth, and letting fly with his left, caught his man under the left eye, drawing blood this time, *sure*. A clinch, and Bell down.

Round 5th. Sully first at it, made

Bell take a brisk circuit to his corner, and when there planted his left handsomely. Bell rushed hotly in, pressed him to the ropes, and by a powerful exertion threw him outside---both down.

Round 5th. Bell a *leetle* excited, commenced warmly, and went in right and left, amid the acclamations of the crowd, keeping Sully, busy stopping, and affording no chance for a return. At last Sully rallied, but it was no go ; Billy forced him back, got in a sounding body blow, and pressed him to the ropes in a close. " Let me go, Billy," said Sullivan, faintly, as he stood with Bell's arm around his neck, at a slight disadvantage near the ropes ; " let me go, Billy ; I can stand it no longer ; I'm a going to give in !" Bell credulously yielded and turned towards his corner, but no sooner had he exposed his unprotected side, than Sullivan let drive a right-handed hit, catching him in the region of the ear. Bell wheeled around and hit short, when he caught it again. A clinch followed, and Sullivan threw him in superb style.

Round 7th. Bell came up with his countenance somewhat " *chafed*,"---the upper part of his dial was quite *eye*-rascible, his nose inflamed, his lip cushioned, and the war paint trickling [though scantily] down his chin. This was Sully's round all through. Bell down.

Round 8th. Sully had it all his own way again until Bell rushed in, and threw him.

Round 9th. Sully led hotly off, menacing mischief; Billy abruptly retreated, and in an attempted rally from the ropes, slipped, and fell.

Round 10th. Beautiful fighting! Sully got in some sounders, which were followed by rapid and heavy exchanges. The Yankee then fibbed him to the ropes, and by a splendid hit, drove him through, clean.

Round 11th. Bell's ogles in bad bread, and his nose bleeding freely. He led off, got in a heavy hit, staved off a sharp rally, clinched, and received a heavy throw

Round 12th.--Bell, with his left ogle nearly closed, and in solemn black, went in well--pressed Sully, who cau-

tiously sparred *away*, but who could not stop the visitation of three or four good blows. Sully rallied, got in a terrifie blow on the eye, and then rushed in both down.

Round 13th.--Both of Bell's peepers nearly closed. Sully led off, but was stopped--a rally--a close--a fierce struggle at the ropes, which ended by Billy throwing his man over.

Round 14th.--Smart exchanges. Bell hitting beautifully right and left, and Sully on the retreat--a wild rush and close by Bell, who caught his man in his arms and tried to heave him over again--no go ; Sully seized the rope, and locked him fast--they were then taken off and carried to their corners, and loud applause for Bell.

Round 15th--All Sullivan's. Bell down heavily.

Round 16th.--Bell came up slow and shy--Sully planted his warlike mauley on Billy's snuff-box, on which Billy closed and was heavily thrown.

Round 17th.---A rally---a clinch--a short struggle at the ropes, and an equal fall over them.

Round 18th.--Ineffective exchanges,-- considerable pantomiming, but nothing done--a clinch, and Bell down.

Round 19th.--Billy led off, but was stopped, and caught a return upon his gory nose--smart exchanges--close, and struggle at the ropes--Sully ending it by tossing him beautifully over.

Round 20th.—It was now apparent to every one, as indeed it had been several rounds before, that Bell could not successfully contend against his experienced adversary. Sully came up smiling, and apparently fresh, while Bell was dreadfully punished, wavering, and unsteady. Sully let fly with his left with terrific effect, completely distracting his enemy, who managed, however, on a rally, to make two or three good but light returns. A clinch, and Bell heavily thrown.

Round 21st.—Bell came up groggy, and scarcely able to see—caught it all over, and in a close was badly thrown.

Round 22d.—Bell failing fast—caught it severely right and left, and went down hopelessly with a stunning blow.

Round 23d.—Bell gone, Sully put in three severe cuts, and Bell went heavily to the ground. Cries of " he's gone!" " Take him out!"

Round 24th.—On time being called, Bell couldn't come, and Sully still fresh, and scarcely hurt, stepped up and claimed the fight, after a contest of 38 minutes.

REMARKS.

Although there was some handsome fighting in the above contest, it cannot be called a good fight Sullivan's qualities and admirable generalship, made it too much on one side. He is a *fighting* man in the true and full sense of the word—light in the scale, and heavy in the field ; strong, agile, quick, cunning, capable, a perfect master of his science; and, if the expression may be used, an intellectual fighter ; for he is continually fighting in his head, and calculating the chances and results of every manœuvre. Bell committed many errors. His first and most gross blunder—and indeed, if he saw Secor's fight, an inexcusable one—was in giving his antagonist *the whole ring.* Instead of fighting on his opponent's ground, and having a clear field to retreat, if necessary, he took a retreating position from the start, suffered himself to be driven in the face of the sun, and forced into a corner on the defensive, in momentary danger of being pressed on the ropes, and thus crippled, " cabined, cribbed, confined," by his own folly, he fought in a 12 foot ring, while his antagonist had a 48 foot one. No experienced general will fight on his own ground if he can help it, and the first inch that Bell gave, when Sullivan was feeling him, exposed his timidity, or, to use a lighter term, his ignorance. Had he presented a determined front, and insisted on a forward movement, he would have kept the sun, retained possession of his ground, changed Sullivan's confidence into caution, and made the fight a longer and better, if not successful one. Bell though a beautiful sparrer, is not a good fighter. He is not equal to emergencies ---seldom follows up his advantages well, and lets many a good opportunity slip. In the third round [if Sully was

not shamming to draw him on] he might have won the fight, instead of which he passed the *profit* to his adversary. Mere weight, strength, and science, do not make the pugilist. Some of the best powers of the prize fighter are in the head. He must have an instinctive love for strife, with the rare accompaniment of a clear, cool, calculating head, and a prompt perception of all the advantages and dangers of his situation. A man does not reason in a situation of imminent danger. He acts upon instinct. " Instinct is a great matter." By the above remarks we do not mean to impugn Bell's courage ; on the contrary, we believe him to be a man of true metal, but of little knowledge. He might have been successful with most any other man of his weight, but is peculiarly unfitted to this antagonist.--- There were other things against him. It was his first fight. The immense concourse was enough to awe and abash him, and, unlike Sullivan, who went to win " sure," he went to win *if he could.*

The defeat of Bell caused great dissatisfaction among his friends, as it was thought he could have won the fight had he followed up his advantages, for it was feared by the backers of Sullivan, while Bell had him on the ropes, that he would be forced to " give in." The stratagem adopted by Sullivan saved him, and assisted materially in changing the whole aspect of the battle. The well-known cunning of his opponent, should have induced Bell not to place any dependance in Sullivan's talk, but should have stimulated him to continue to punish his man whilst he had him in his power. Had he done so, the victory would have been with him. Once out of the uncomfortable position in which he had been placed, Sullivan felt himself a new man, and his lucky escape made him more cautious in regard to his future movements, and he felt satisfied that he could easily win, having fully ascertained the weak points of his adversary.

The opponents of Sullivan were now in no better luck than before the battle, and they were at a loss where to look for a champion, for they were bound to "take down" the Yankee. The fighting fever was at its height, at this time, and great excitement was manifested as to the coming fight between Lilly and McCoy. The battle between Sullivan and Bell took place on the 29th of August, 1842, and the fight between Lilly and McCoy was announced to take place on the 13th of September, just two weeks after. The victory of Sullivan gave increased confidence to the friends and backers of McCoy, more especially as Sullivan lent his aid and experience in bringing McCoy forward in good condition, and instilling into his mind many little bits of advice which he knew would be useful to McCoy on the battle field.

The friends of Lilly were not idle. They used every exertion to train him " in the way he should go," and as the result proved, their attention had not been thrown away.

Lilly and McCoy met at Hastings, up the North River, on the 13th of September, 1842, and after a sharply contested battle of 2 hours and 43 minutes, in which time one hundred and nineteen rounds were fought, time was called for the combatants to begin the 120th round, but McCoy was deaf to the call—he was stretched upon the ground in the agonies of death, and there within the prize-ring, and with his young companions around him, unable to render him any assistance, he suffered the severest tortures, and after lingering for about fifteen minutes, he passed from life into

eternity. The vast assemblage became panic-struck, and each one seemed anxious to leave the spot.

In a short time, the scene of this fatal and terrifying encounter was left to its usual quietude, and no one would have supposed that this beautiful spot of ground had been stained by the blood of a human-being.

Lilly succeeded in making his escape, but Sullivan, who was on the ground during the fight, was in a short time after arrested, and after being tried as an accessory to the murder of McCoy, he was convicted by the authorities of West-chester County, the county in which the battle was fought, and was subsequently sentenced to an imprisonment of two years. Part of this time he served out, but through the intercession of his friends, the Governor of New York granted him a pardon, on condition that he would engage in no more prize-fights.

Prize fighting, owing to the fatal termination of the Lilly and McCoy fight, was thus brought to a full stop, for a long time, at least ; and most of the fraternity were compelled to leave for parts unknown. A few years, however, sufficed to calm the public mind, and as Sullivan had been pardoned, and further proceedings in reference to the fatal fight quashed, the absentees regained confidence, and one by one returned to the great Empire City. Lilly did not return, but kept out of the way, and on the 15th of January, 1847, turned up at Natchez, where he had a battle with an English pugilist named Harris Birchall. They fought for $500 a side, and Birchall was defeated in 27 rounds, occupying 55 minutes. Several other battles had taken place, and as Sullivan had kept quiet a number of years, it was thought all remembrance of the past had been forgotten. Accordingly, about the commencement of the year 1847 an English pugilist named Robert Caunt, brother to the English Champion, Ben Caunt, who had been in this country a short time, attracted the attention of the Sullivan party, and as it was supposed Caunt would afford a fair chance for the display of Sullivan's tactics, a match was concluded in the month of January, between the famous Yankee Sullivan and the English Champion's brother. Immense sums of money were wagered on the result of the contest, not only in this country, but throughout Great Britain, where the remembrance of Sullivan's fight with Hammer Lane had rendered him notorious. In England it was confidently hoped and expected that the younger Caunt would be able to wipe out the stain caused by the defeat of the great Hammer Lane. In this country the feeling was rather in favor of Sullivan, as he fought under the name of "Yankee," and thus enlisted the sympathies of the people. The Sons of Erin, however, were in extacies at the prospect of a fight between one of their own countrymen and an Englishman, and were no way slow in backing their favorite to the last copper in their possession. The annexed report we copy from the New York Herald, of May 14, 1847.

The Prize Fight of Sullivan and Caunt for $300.

This affair, which has caused so much excitement in the sporting world for the last four months, both in this country and Great Britain, was decided on Tuesday last, May 11th, in the neighborhood of Harper's Ferry, Virginia.

For several days previous to the fight numbers of strange faces were noticed in the vicinity, and the curiosity of the inhabitants to know what brought them thither, was brought to the highest pitch of excitement. Caunt and his seconds had arrived there a few days previous to the contest, with a view of examining the localities and conciliating the people, as opposition to such proceedings was anticipated. They found very little opposition however, as the residents were all anxious to witness the sport, and it became the leading topic of conversation among all classes of society, who waited with anxiety to witness a man fight on the improved English system.

On the arrival of the railroad train at the depot on Monday, hundreds of the patrons of the fistic art left the cars, and were seen moving in every direction through the town, endeavoring to secure abodes for the coming night, which they found no easy matter.

As night came on, crowds began to congregate about the Hotels, and speculate on the events that were to be enacted on the subsequent day. At nine o'clock the crowd dispersed, the Virginians to their homes, and the Strangers to seek the beds they had previously engaged (which by the by, had been let and re-let by their owners as often as they were applied for), or to take the chances of securing those belonging to other individuals. The scarcity of the accommodations was so great that as often as many as ten persons were crowded into a small room, while on the floors of the parlors any quantity were stretched out.

As soon as day dawned on the morning of the 11th, the people began to turn out and assemble about the doors of the hotel, to ascertain where the battle was to be fought, although it was raining tremendously at the time, fearful of disappointment in not witnessing the affair. The ground had been selected the night previous, and both parties had agreed to fight at an early hour in the day. It had been understood by the principals that the commandant of the armory intended to interfere and stop the proceeding, supposing that they had chosen the ground for that purpose in Jefferson county; which would take the workmen in the foundries away from their occupations, and being then determined to prevent it, he procured a warrant for the belligerents. This was ascertained from some of the peace officials of the neighborhood, who were themselves anxious to witness a pugilistic encounter of the latest fashion. The commissaries were started on a tour of exploration into Lowden county, the next adjoining, in search of a battle field, out of the jurisdiction of Jefferson county. They soon returned, and announced that they had found a suitable place, where the civil authorities would offer no obstacles, as they were inclined to witness the latest improvements of this kind of warfare—the science not having yet reached Virginia. This intelligence was received by all parties with much satisfaction, and by eight o'clock all were on the march for the scene of action.

The ground selected for the fight was in a beautiful meadow, as level as a parlor floor, at the foot of one of the Blue Ridge mountains, the Potomac river circling round it. On the opposite side of the Potomac was the State of Maryland, which, in case of a visit from the peace-makers, might be reached in a few moments, the river being fordable at that point, and business renewed and settled before the majesty of the law could be apprised of the pugilistic proceedings of their uninvited visitors.

The stakes were pitched soon after eight o'clock, both parties being anxious to have the affair over at an early hour, so that they might be able to depart in the twelve o'clock train. A twenty-four feet ring was erected, around which there was an outer one about two hundred feet in circumference.

The assemblage placed themselves in an orderly manner around the outer ring, a few countrymen acting as ring keepers, and appearing disposed to do everything in their power to ensure fair play and good order.

There were a number of small houses at the base of the mountain, the roofs and porches of which were filled with anxious gazers; and away up the mountains, as far as the eye could discern, were seen human beings, who were endeavoring to witness the performances, without being themselves recognized by their neighbors; their natural inclinations leading them to witness scenes which their position in society compelled them publicly to denounce.

There were probably six or seven hundred spectators, altogether, who came from all parts of the United States, some of whom had travelled three thousand miles to witness the fight.

Everything being in readiness, the combatants were called for, the spectators not being willing to stand in the rain longer than necessary. Sullivan was the first to make his appearance on the ground, when he threw his cap into the ring, following it, and sitting down on the knee of one of his seconds, apparently anxious to get at work. In a few minutes Caunt approached the ring, and hurled in his hat, stepped over the ropes, walked up to Sullivan, and shook hands with him; after which he took his seat on the opposite side of the ring. Sullivan's weight was 150 pounds; Caunt's, 164 pounds. The former was waited upon by Tom O'Donnel and John Lyng, and Caunt by James Sanford and Mason Bennett. The betting on the ground was very limited, notwithstanding the great odds offered on Sullivan, 100 to 40 being the standard. There were a few bets that Sullivan would win it in less than an hour.

The preliminaries being settled, at three minutes after nine o'clock the men commenced stripping off their unnecessary apparel, and their respective colors were hung up, that of Sullivan being green, while that of Caunt was blue, with white spots. All being ready, Caunt asked Sullivan if they had not better begin; when both men, with their seconds, came to the scratch, shook hands, [ten minutes after nine o'clock,] went back to their respective corners, and awaited the call of time for

THE FIGHT.

Round 1st. At the call of time, both men walked to the scratch, and put themselves into positions of defence; but Sullivan was so eager to commence work, that he crossed the line, and walked up to Caunt, his hands well up. As he reached Caunt, the latter stepped back, at the same time hitting out with his left hand, which fell lightly on the breast of Sullivan, and then took another back step, Sullivan following. Sullivan hit with his left, which Caunt stopped very finely; but Sullivan stepped in closer to him, and succeeded in planting a sharp hit on his mouth, which started the blood in profusion. (First blood was claimed for him by his seconds) Caunt had by this time reached the ropes near his corner and he made an effort to fight his way out: he struck out left and right at Sullivan's head. The most of his blows were stopped, and those that reached home made but very little impression, the blows of the other party telling at every effort. They then fought to a close, when Sullivan succeeded in getting him on his hip, and threw him heavily, falling upon him. (This event, so much unexpected, dampened the hopes of Caunt's friends, they relying much on his wrestling capabilities.) The round was a very short one, and the work on both sides very sharp, but much in favor of Sullivan.

Round 2nd.—At the call of time, the men sprang quickly up from the knees of their seconds, and hastened to the scratch, which Sullivan again crossed, and made up to Caunt, from whose mouth blood was running rapidly. Caunt led off as Sullivan approached him, and fought away with his left and right hands; Sullivan rushing after him stopping his blows, and dealing out in return some of his beauty destroyers. They then drew apart for a moment, came up again for mischief, Caunt this time stopping cleverly a number of Sullivan's tremendous hits; Caunt retreated, striking Sullivan twice on the head, and taking a couple of hard ones in return. They made a turn round, Sullivan's back coming near the ropes ; and as he rushed at Caunt, apparently full of venom, and determined to make the fight as short as possible, Caunt managed to get his right hand to tell on his head, staggering him for a moment to

the ropes ; but Caunt did not follow him in time to profit by this advantage, for Sullivan recovered himself, and was at him again, shooting in his left and right fearfully, on the face of Caunt, who fought on, doing all he knew, until they closed; when in the struggle for the fall, Sullivan fell through the ropes, and Caunt hung on them. (The ropes were very loose, and gave way so easily that Sullivan might rather attribute his fall to them, than to any manœuvring of his opponent.) Sullivan had a great advantage in this round, and it was manifest that he was so much superior to Caunt as a fighter, that the chances of the latter were small, without an accident. If the odds were 100 to 40 at the commencement, they were now 100 to 10, so much advantage had Sullivan already gained.

Round 3rd.—As soon as time was up, Sullivan jumped from his second's knees and quickly walked to the scratch. Caunt likewise appeared in a hurry ; and as soon as they got in hitting distance, fighting commenced, when some very fine stopping was made by both parties. Caunt would hit and retreat, Sullivan rapidly following him and nailing him severely in the face, which was swelling very fast, and the blood flowing out of the openings very freely. They struck three times together, counter hits, in the face ; Sullivan's blows were very hard, while those of Caunt, except the first one, amounted almost to nothing ; the first one, however, did make a slight opening on Sullivan's forehead. A rally then ensued and Sullivan threw Caunt and fell beside him. Caunt's face was now dreadfully mangled ; the left cheek puffed up to an immense size, and a hole under the right eye was visible that had been made in this round ; in fact, a more severe and effective round has been seldom witnessed, and all agreed that this round was the best and sharpest that they ever saw Sullivan fight. All were surprised at his skill and activity. He made some joking remarks during the round about Caunt's appearance, but they were not much heeded by the other. It appeared to all that there was no chance for Caunt, and his friends began to despair. An accident was his only hope.

Round 4th.—The word "time" had hardly passed from the lips when Sullivan was on his feet and at the scratch, determined to make short work of it. Caunt came up,too,evidently determined to do something to try and turn the tide which was setting strongly against him. He rushed at Sullivan and was met with a flush left-handed hit on the upper lip, and a hard right-hander on the side of the head; but nothing daunted, he dashed out both hands, hitting Sullivan twice, although without much damage. A sharp rally then ensued, and as they closed, Sullivan slipped his foothold and fell on the ground, Caunt, on his feet, standing over him: he then turned and walked over to his seconds. (The head of Caunt was by this time very much disfigured, and he appeared to be somewhat stupified from the tremendous hits he had received on the side of his head). In this round he made a desperate lunge with his right hand at Sullivan's body, but Sullivan dropped his arm and stopped it. The blow cracked like a whip, and had it reached its destination it would undoubtedly have done considerable damage. Nothing had occurred thus far to revive the drooping fortune of Caunt, and it seemed more and more certain, that the sooner the fight was brought to a close, the safer it would be for the parties interested.

Round 5th.—On coming to the scratch this round, Sullivan fell back, evidently to draw Caunt after him, but it would not do: he then went up and hit at him and as soon as Caunt made fight he retreated again, when finding these tactics did not take, he came up and dashed away at his opponent, who in turn gave way, Sullivan following him and punishing him severely. Caunt turned his head to spit out some blood, which Sullivan took advantage of and struck him a tremendous hit on the front of the face, and rushed at him with his left and righ-handers, hitting very severely. Caunt rallied and caught Sullivan on the left cheek, and another hit on the side of the head. Sullivan dashed at him, Caunt retreated with his hands very low down, and appeared for the moment to forget what his business was in the ring: his seconds shouting at him, he roused himself. Sullivan fought him to the ropes, where, in a rally and close, both of them, from the loose manner the ropes were put up, fell over on the outer side. Both men were quickly picked up and carried to their respective corners. Caunt now seemed in a state of bewilderment; his head had been so often and so severely hit that it . was no wonder that he was stupid, and some of his friends who thought more of the man than they did of the money they had staked on him, wished the affair brought to a close.

Round 6th.—At the call of time, Sullivan was quickly on his feet, making a rush to meet Caunt, and as soon as he got near him he went to work with both hands, Caunt giving some and taking much. Sullivan rushed in so desperately at Caunt—who kept backing out, hitting as he retreated, his blows when they did reach, doing but little injury—that he gave him no time to consider what to do ; he drove him to the ropes. where they had a struggle, and Sullivan, supposing he had knocked him down, turned to go to his corner ; but his attention being called to Caunt, who had staggered to the ropes and who was leaning on them apparently unconscious, he rushed back and made a terrific lunge at Caunt with his left, which Caunt dodged : Sullivan struck him with his left hand, and Caunt got hold of him, and they had a struggle and both went down. (The fighting in this round was even more severe than any of the others, and the rapidity with which Sullivan fought astonished his most sanguine friends, even those who believe that his match is not in the world of his weight. At the end of the round there was a burst of applause from all sides of the ring, the country people joining in.)

Round 7th.—As Caunt rose from the knees of his second, he appeared unsteady on his feet, while, on the contrary, Sullivan seemed as fresh and vigorous as he was at the beginning—and as he came near Caunt he laughed at him, and said something about the damaged condition of his face. This seemed to arouse Caunt, who opened the fight, and at it they went, hit for hit, Sullivan driving him before him all round the ring until they reached the corner where the umpires were stationed, where Sullivan backed Caunt on the ropes; and the hitting on both sides here was very sharp, but that of Caunt was not strong enough to beat him back, and Sullivan punished him dreadfully. They then closed and had a struggle on the ropes, both of them hanging over them, doing nothing for a moment; after which they got away again, and Caunt put his leg around Sullivan's to throw him, holding him, at the same time around the neck with his left hand. Sullivan endeavored to extricate himself, and in the effort Caunt fell, and " foul " was shouted out by the second of Caunt, and one of the umpires; "fair," shouted the other umpire, and the referee was appealed to. During this confusion the word time was called by a dozen voices, and Sullivan went up to the scratch to renew the fight, and called for Caunt to come up; but Caunt's friends ordered him not to move from his place, that he had won the fight. Sullivan's attendants, after waiting about sixteen seconds, took him in their arms and passed him out of the ring, claiming the fight for him.

At this time a rush was made around the umpires; and the reporter, believing that in the melee other bumps might be added to his head than the already largely developed one of caution, made the best of his way out of the throng, and there awaited the issue. The fight being ended, he repaired to the referee and asked his decision, when he replied, " Sullivan has won the fight."

The fight lasted exactly twelve minutes.

The battle between Caunt and Sullivan terminated in a manner somewhat similar to the recent fight between Morrissey and Sullivan. That Sullivan had the best of the battle certainly none can deny. Caunt disappointed the hopes of his friends, who had expected much better skill in the art, than he displayed. Sullivan on the contrary, seemed well up to the mark, and showed his superiority over his more weighty opponent.

There was a cessation of hostilities at this time between the members of the pugilistic fraternity, owing to the commencement of the preliminary arrangements for a grand set-to between Uncle Sam and John Mexico. Those who had been enemies in the ring before, were now anxious to stand up together in behalf of Uncle Sam, who had always been a father to them. Sullivan, however, still kept the " fight" in him, expecting, no doubt that he would be called upon, after the war excitement was over, to have "another little brush." There was a bad feeling existing between the Sullivan party and the Hyer party, more especially since the defeat of Country McCleester by the youthful, though rather dangerous pugilist, Tom Hyer. The friends of Sullivan seemed eager to bring the respective conquerers of Caunt and McCleester into competition in the ring, to see which was the best man. Hyer had no desire to fight, yet was "always ready" to take his own part and assist a friend when needed. As he had before stated his unwillingness to enter the ring for a mere paltry sum of a few hundred dollars, he still adhered to that determination, and all efforts to induce him to change his mind were fruitless. Sullivan was anxious for an opportunity to meet "Young America," but the amount of money necessary to raise before the match could be made operated against him, and he was forced to let matters rest for the time. It was evident, however, that the different parties could not exist in such a state of uncertainty, and numerous little battles almost daily took place between the friends of both men. From this time out it was nothing but talk, talk, talk, as to the respective merits of Hyer and Sullivan. Sullivan at this time kept a public house at No. 9 Chatham street. The National Police Gazette, to which paper we are indebted for the particulars of the great contest between Hyer and Sullivan, says, in speaking of Sullivan, and of the first meeting of the men, that the spirit of the gladiator was still strong within him, [Sullivan,] and he could not restrain himself from looking awry at Hyer whenever he came in contact with him, nor of indicating, in various significant ways, that, notwithstanding that individual's size, his youth, and length of reach, he could " flax him out with very little difficulty." In this spirit, and what was worse, with too much spirit in him, he one evening in April, 1848, dropped into the splendid restaurant on the corner of Broadway and Park Place, and being off his guard with the foolish liquor in him, gave Hyer [who was somewhat in the same condition] such provocation that an immediate fight ensued. The story was soon told. The conqueror of Hammer Lane, and theretofore invincible Sullivan, was beaten into insensibility, and taken out of the cellar, leaving Hyer cock of the walk.

It is scarcely possible to describe the excitement which this event occasioned in the public mind. For five or six days, nothing else was talked of in all circles, and for the corresponding nights Broadway swarmed with the crowds which concentrated from all quarters of the town to catch a glance, while parading from one drinking house to another,

of the man who had whipped Yankee Sullivan. The papers teemed with the event, and the general expression seemed one of gratification at the result. Sullivan's friends, however, took strong objections to the manner in which his overthrow had been accomplished, and insisted that he had been taken at a hopeless disadvantage. The other side recriminated, of course, that such a complaint was a mere vain pretence.

In the meantime both factions armed themselves, and for a period of five weeks, there was a momentary dread in the minds of the peace loving, that several lives would be lost by the collision of the parties. It seems, however, that Mr. Sullivan took a second sober thought, and being averse to bowie knives or shooting irons, he concluded to dictate a personal challenge, and to that end and purpose, sent the following card to the New York Herald, which was published in that journal, on Wednesday, the first of June, 1848.

A CARD.

About six weeks since, while in the saloon on the corner of Park Place and Broadway, in a condition rendering me unable to defend myself against any attack, I was assailed in a most cowardly manner, by a man of the name of Hyer. On the strength of it, accounts of the occurrence appeared in a number of the newspapers, false in every particular, and which must have been inserted by Hyer himself, or his friends. If I had been worsted in a fair fight, and by a person who knew anything at all about fighting, or had the courage to fight as a man, I should have taken no notice of it ; but I consider it due to my friends, to inform them in this way of the real character of the occurrence. I am no " Irish braggart" or " bully," although I am an Irishman, and believe I can show myself worthy of my country whenever I am required. If there are any who think they can make me "cry enough, like a whipped child," if No. 9 Chatham street is not too far out of the way, I will be happy to have them call and make the experiment. As for Hyer, I can "flax him out" without any exertion.

JAMES SULLIVAN.

On the following day, Thursday, the 2d of June, 1848, the following brief reply to the above card was published in the Herald.

● A REPLY.

Yesterday morning it was falsely stated in one of the advertisements of this paper, signed "James Sullivan," that I had assailed him in an unjustifiable manner, and at a disadvantage, about six weeks ago, in a saloon at the corner of Park Place and Broadway. I wish merely to state, that this fellow, Sullivan, assaulted me, and that I chastised him for it, as I can and shall do again on similar provocation, to him or any one else who improperly assails me. I have only to add, that Mr. Sullivan will find me always much readier to meet him anywhere than in the newspapers ; anywhere, however, I am his master. THOMAS HYER.

These two letters, though sufficiently belligerent in their tone, did not lead immediately to the arrangement to which both parties seemed desirous to come, and two months more elapsed in hostile traversing, in the hope to catch each other in some chance melee. In the first week in August, however, a bar-room banter to Hyer, of $20, by one of Sullivan's adherents, to the effect that he dared not make a match with Sullivan, produced the requisite arrangement. Hyer put up the twenty dollars, and, in pursuance of the conditions of the wager, a meeting was had at Ford's tavern, at No. 28 Park Row, by the friends and backers of both parties, on the night of Monday, 7th August. To win the twenty dollar banter, therefore, Hyer stood ready to make a match for $10,000, or $5,000 a side, and put down $100 as a temporary forfeit. Though the offer of such a tremendous stake seemed to stagger the friends of Sullivan not a little, they nevertheless came boldly up to the scratch, and the match was at once agreed on.

As soon as this ceremony was over, the following articles of agreement were drawn up, or produced, and being duly executed, became from that hour the law for the contest :—

Articles of Agreement

Entered into this seventh day of August, 1848, between James Sullivan and Thomas Hyer.

RULES TO BE GOVERNED BY.

The said James Sullivan agrees to fight the said Thomas Hyer a fair stand up fight, half minute time, in a twenty-four feet roped ring, according to the new rules as laid down in the Fistiana for 1848, by which rules the said Sullivan and Hyer hereby mutually agree to be bound.

AMOUNT OF STAKE AND PLACE OF FIGHT.

The said fight shall be for the sum of *Five Thousand Dollars* aside. The said fight shall take place within the states of Virginia or Maryland, or some other place, if the parties can mutually agree upon such other place.

TO INCREASE OR LESSEN THE STAKE.

The fight can be made for a greater or lesser sum than Five Thousand Dollars aside, by mutual consent of the parties.

WITHIN SIX MONTHS.

The said fight shall take place within six months from the date of these articles.

HOURS BETWEEN WHICH THE FIGHT SHALL TAKE PLACE.

On the day on which the fight takes place, each man shall be in the ring on or before 1 o'clock P. M., or at an earlier hour if the parties mutually agree.

PROVISION AGAINST INTERFERENCE.

In case of magisterial interference or other interruption of the fight, which the umpires shall deem fair cause for adjourning the fight, the referee or stake holder shall name the time and place for the next meeting of the parties to decide or terminate the fight.

Each man shall be attired suitably for fair ring fighting.

NO ADVANTAGE.

No unfair shoes or unfair means shall be resorted to during the fight or at the termination thereof.

AGREEMENT TO GIVE NO INFORMATION.

It is hereby agreed, that no information shall be given to any person, whereby the authorities may interfere to stop the fight.

CHOICE OF GROUND.

The party winning the choice of ground for fighting, shall give the other party ten days' notice of the place selected for the fight, such information to be fair and unequivocal as to its whereabouts.

CONVEYANCE TO GROUND.

Should it be necessary to employ a steamboat to convey the parties and their friends to the place of fighting, and a steamboat be chartered, the proceeds of such boat shall be equally divided between the parties.

FIRST INSTALMENT.

Five Hundred Dollars aside (making One Thousand Dollars) are now deposited in the hands of J— B— F—, in pursuance of the foregoing agreement.

SECOND INSTALMENT.

The next deposit of *Five Hundred Dollars* aside to be put up at the house of James Sullivan, No. 9 Chatham street, in the hands of J. B. F., on Monday evening, 21st of August, between the hours of 8 and 10 P. M.

THIRD INSTALMENT.

On the 21st day of September, *Seven Hundred and Fifty Dollars* aside to be put up at the house of Ford & Phillips, 28 Park Row.

FOURTH INSTALMENT.

On the 21st day of October, Seven Hundred and Fifty Dollars aside at No. 9 Chatham street

FIFTH INSTALMENT.

On the 21st day of November, Seven Hundred and Fifty Dollars a side, to be put up at No. 28 Park Row.

SIXTH INSTALMENT.

On the 21st of day December, Seven Hundred and Fifty Dollars aside, to be put up at No. 9 Chatham street.

The above mentioned deposits of Seven Hundred and Fifty Dollars aside, to be put up at the places described between the hours of 8 and 10 P. M.

FINAL INSTALMENT.

The last and final deposit of One Thousand Dollars aside, to be put up at 28 Park Row on the 8th day of January, 1849, between the hours of 8 and 10 P. M.

FORFEIT.

Either party failing to comply with the above conditions, shall forfeit the money already down.

STAKEHOLDER.

All the sums above mentioned, to be put up in the hands of J— B— F—, who shall be empowered, in case of his sickness or absence from the city, to name or appoint a person to receive for him the deposits.

RULES TO UMPIRES.

Each party shall furnish their respective umpires with a copy of " Fistiana."

NO ADVANTAGES.

It is distinctly understood that no undue advantage shall be taken by either party ; but every transaction shall take place in a fair business-like manner

REFEREE.

Each party shall choose an umpire, and they, the umpires, shall choose a referee, whose decision shall be final and binding upon the parties.

STAKES.

The stakes not to be given up until fairly won or lost, by a fight or by forfeiture. In pursuance of this agreement, the parties hereunto attach their names

Signed,   F. M. for
                     JAMES SULLIVAN.
                     M. M. for
                     THOS. HYER.

Witness—A. N. }
       T. C. B. }

These arrangements having been made, and ratified with a general bumper of champagne, the parties separated, and the public drew a long breath of relief at having escaped the danger of a street slaughter which had so long been threatened. The interest having now taken a temperate and a legitimate direction, rose higher than ever, and with the New York community, divided the excitement caused by the approaching Presidential campaign. Both men, and the backers of both, in the meanwhile seemed to feel the highest confidence in their respective causes, the best evidence of which lies in the fact of the promptness and regularity with which the instalments of the monster wager were put up. The long period set for the training excited some surprise in the general mind, but to the initiated it was considered necessary, in order to correct the irregularities of Hyer's mode of life, and as an indulgence, which Sullivan on his part required, so that he might take, for a while, the light and gentle discipline requisite to a man who had trained so often before.

The men immediately made arrangements for training, &c., and as the reporter for the Gazette gave a very faithful report of the doings of each we give his report verbatim. The first is a description of a sparring exhibition given by Yankee Sullivan in the month succeeding the making of the match. We have struck from it the intermediate set-to's, and have retained only what will serve to give a graphic idea of the spirit in which everything appertaining to the fight was conducted, and what relates personally to the principals.

September 30th, 1848.

Excitement among the Fighting Crowd.

SULLIVAN'S EXHIBITION.—According to the custom of distinguished pugilists when fitted against each other for a fight, each of the main parties to the contest, gives, during the period of training, three or four sparring exhibitions, that he may test the good-will of his friends, and display his condition to those who have laid, or who wish to lay, their money out upon him. Following the principals, come the seconds and the trainers, who, however, having less claim upon the curiosity of the public, content themselves with a "benefit" a piece, and with considerate deference usually charge but half the price required by their employers.

In accordance with these regulations. as ancient and invariable as the laws of the Medes and Persians, James, otherwise Yankee Sullivan, on Monday night last, gave a "grand" exhibition at the Shakespeare Hotel, price 50 cents a head, at which the most famous of the "fancy" regaled each other, in couples, with a series of friendly punches in the head. We were there; so were some eight hundred distinguished persons, in the shape of editors, doctors, lawyers, brokers, clerks, exquisites, philosophers, (no Clergymen who were identified as such), and swarms of the boys and "hitters out," filling the huge ball-room with multifarious and grotesque intelligence, even to the little music perch, stuck on one of the side walls.

The performances of the evening were of an exciting character. Barring the first set-to, in which two Chatham street Jews puffed each other's faces with square-handed smacks, the contests were spirited and in many cases severe.

At the commencement of the next display the room was entered by a celebrated sporting editor, accompanied by some dozen of his friends, among whom was the Honorable John M. Botts and a commodore of the navy, who, walking across the room at a step something brisker than the dead march in Saul, melted down among the front row of squatters, who cottoned to the floor, on the furtherest side.

During the progress of this set-to, Hyer, who is matched against Sullivan for $10,000, and Thompson his trainer, entered the room, and, for a few moments, engrossed the attention of all who were in their neighbourhood.

Hyer already shows the improvement of his brief training, since the making of the match. He is a tall, splendid looking fellow, of some six feet two inches in height, with—regular and handsome features and a form that is a happy combination of Hercules and the Apollo Belvidere. His countenance is strikingly American, while that of his trainer, who is a man of almost equally formidable dimensions, is no less decidedly English. As for Sullivan, the Emerald Isle never had a more unmistakeable specimen of her hardy race.

After three more set-to's, the last of which was a brisk and severe one, between a Frenchman and the famous Awful Gardner, Sullivan and Thompson, duly prepared for sharp work, entered the arena, accompanied by the celebrated Country M'Cluskey, who, amidst repeated showers of applause, introduced them to the company. Country then retired, and the skilful combatants then squared for each other amid the most breathless silence of the before tumultuous crowd. Sullivan looked the perfect beau ideal of a fighting man. He was dressed in the complete uniform of the ring, and, as he confronted his antagonist, with his keen mischievous eye riveted upon him, we never saw anything more striking than the deeply earnest expression of his peculiar physiognomy. Contrasted with Sullivan, Thompson, who is over six feet high, looked like a young giant, and his skill and action, proved to be no less formidable, than in his muscular powers.

As the combatants measured each other's reach, Hyer looked over the heads of the crowd and studied every motion of Thompson's antagonist, with the intense attention which befitted a man who was to oppose his powers to

those of the latter for $10,000.

The combatants advanced and retreated; they alternately changed sides, and then cautiously worked back to their first positions : they feinted, took guard, smiled at the failures of each, and again grew serious, when, of a sudden, Sullivan let fly with his left, and planted his glove full upon his opponent's nose, and having gained this advantage, he got away and closed the round. As this artistic blow was given, loud cheers were given by Sullivan's friends from all parts of the room. In the next round Thompson showed the most admirable skill, dealing Sullivan some tremendous counter-hits, as well as several gratuitous discharges, which kept the Champion continually at work. In the third round, Thompson endeavored to maintain the same tactics, and drove Sullivan to the edge of the spectators, when the latter suddenly closed and threw him handsomely, landing him upon his shoulder. This superb manœuvre occasioned the most vociferous applause on the part of Sullivan's friends, some of whom rushed into the ring and tossed their hats up to the ceiling in their ecstacy.

On coming to the scratch in the next round, Thompson looked feverish. He commenced the round most wickedly, and leading off, hit out right and left, driving Sullivan by his headlong and irresistable advance, among the spectators. Perceiving now, that the thing had become too earnest for sport, Sullivan, with proper judgment, bowed to the audience and would have ended the contest; but Thompson, who wished to get an offset for "that throw," waved him back, and the audience seconded the proposition with such unanimous voice, that Sullivan could not resist the challenge. Mischief now flashed from the eyes of each, and soon sharp exchanges rung on the heads of both. Seizing a chance, Thompson rushed in impetuously and grasped the champion, and rather by main strength than by the exercise of any other quality, gave him a lance throw among the spectators. Just as this feat was accomplished, some one of Sullivan's friends, irritated at what he conceived to be a momentary

discomfiture of his favorite, either kicked Thompson, or made an overture to do
so ; whereupon a member of the opposition called the hon. gentleman to order
by seizing him by the coller, and threatening to "mortify his jaw." This was
the signal for a general rush, and in the
close of bodies and the strife of arms,
there was for some minutes the pros-
pect of a terrible melee. We have seldom witnessed a more exciting scene,
and more than once, it seemed that the
rival factions, which adhered respect-
ively to Hyer and Sullivan, were about
to settle in the presence of their leaders,
and out of hand, the original difficulty
which gave rise to their present match.
By the judicious efforts of some influen-
tial peace-makers, however, quiet was
at length restored, and the evening's
business wound up by a severe glove
fight between Tom O'Donnel, the trainer
of Sullivan, and an excellent sparrer
named Mike Kelly.

In order to make the history of the
great match between Hyer and Sullivan as complete as possible, we here-
with present for the consideration of
our readers, the particulars of the Sparring Exhibition for the benefit of Hyer.
It is the second of the series of papers
before referred to :

November 23d, '48 }
The third month }

GRAND MEETING OF THE FANCY.

HYER'S EXHIBITION.—The " grand "
sparring exhibition of Tom Hyer, which
we predicted some time ago, " came
off," to use a sporting term, on Friday
evening last, at Mager's ball-room, in
Elizabeth street. To our surprise we
found, on entering the room, which is a
very large one, that it was densely filled with spectators of every class, the
nearer circles of which stood closely
wedged around an elevated staging,
and the outer edges swarmed upwards
on chance elevations balancing themselves by holding on each other's shoulders. At eight o'clock, the impatience
of the audience rather elegantly expressed in various modes of sounds,

summoned forth two of the athletæ,
who, arrayed in the fighting garb,
jumped into the twenty-four feet roped
elevated ring, and made their obeisance
to the audience.

The combatants were the veteran
George Kensett, the hero of several
fights, and a young man named McKay.
Though much heavier than the pugilistic sage, the stalwart Mr. McKay was
obliged to receive the compliment of a
bloody mouth from one of the veteran's
right hand hits, and to receive a succession of similar attentions, beautifully
delivered in the same favored place.

* * * * * *

Bob Sauce and McStravick, an English prize-fighter, were the next. The
latter of these men, though evidently a
very excellent sparrer, did not attempt
to work, but gave his more inexperienced
adversary the advantage from first to
last. His object showed itself after a
few rounds, when, leaning up against
the ropes, as if almost overcome with
faintness and fatigue, he gave utterance
to the following delectable rhetorical
display :—

" Gentlemen, I doant feel so well to-
noight ; but I'll fight any man in the
country nor doant weigh no more nor
I'm stun."

" Come here, my laddy ; we've got a
match for your ten stone man," said the
honorable Mr. Closey, a member from
one of upper districts ; whereat Mr. Mc-
Stravick moved toward Mr. Closey, to
settle the preliminaries. This affair
being disposed of according to the laws
in such cases made and provided, and
Tom O'Donnell being understood as
the accepting candidate, the sports went
on.

* * * * * *

TOM HYER AND GEORGE THOMPSON.
The appearance of these men in the
ring created the deepest sensation ; and
while they put themselves in position,
and squared cautiously away, the most
profound silence reigned through the
crowded auditory. As both of the men
are some two or three inches above six
feet, and both also in the pride of youth
and strength, it was an exceedingly interesting sight as they confronted each

other, with a severe and earnest watchfulness. It appeared to us that Hyer's position, though handsome, was rather stiff and inclined too much backwards; while Thompson's was well forward, and easy, and ready for all sorts of work. The combatants sparred cautiously for some time, both careful and proud of their reputations, and several moments elapsed before either would venture to break ground. At length, however, watching his chance, Hyer let fly a straight right-handed hit, and delivered his glove full upon Thompson's chin, with a sharpness that sent the color tingling to the skin, and with a power that would have driven an ordinary man through the ropes among the audience. Best of all, he recovered in an instant, and got away from a mischievously meant return. A full round of applause manifested itself at this for Hyer, and while it was yet ringing, the gigantic adversary squared for the second round. In this round it was blow for blow; and so it kept throughout a twenty minutes' contest, Hyer displaying a good style of hitting and an equal degree of skill in stopping his opponent's blows. His best point, and the one that will most bestead him in his coming fight with Sullivan, is his tact in countering; he seeming to have made it his especial study to give a blow invariably, for every one he is obliged to take. This is an invaluable rule for combatants who have the largest powers of endurance, as in blow for blow, the weakest structure shivers and leaves the strongest master of the field. We were surprised, however, to see Hyer perspire so freely with his efforts. The sweat ran from him like rain, and told a tale of careless training which created evident uneasiness in the faces of his backers.

———

December 3d, 1848 }
The 4th month. }

TRAINING FOR THE FIGHT.

YANKEE SULLIVAN.

Since the grand sparring exhibition recently given by Tom Hyer, that distinguished individual and his famous opponent, Yankee Sullivan, have put themselves in active training for the desperate fight which is to come off between them for the sum of $10,000, on teh 7th of February next. Hyer, with his two trainers, Thompson and Joe Winrow, has taken up his field quarters at Dodge's, at McComb's Dam, and Sullivan, attended by the celebrated Country McCleester and Tom O'Donnell, rusticate at Shaw's, hard by the Union Race Course, on Long Island. Of the two places, Hyer has much the best of it, the adjacent country furnishing fine rugged hills for him to climb and struggle over, while Sullivan has not much at his command beside the flat race-course, and such variety as he can manufacture out of low sandy ground, or by feats of picking up stones at a full run.

As the mode of training taken for the development of the highest perfection of the animal health and strength in man cannot be otherwise than interesting and instructive, we will give the routine of Sullivan's exercises and mode of living. We do it more willingly as he disclaims any intention of preparing himself for a fight, proclaiming his object solely to be to train against the coming Cholera, by a purification of his system. He doubtless will be properly prepared to meet it.

In the morning the Hon. Mr. Sullivan rises with the first streak of dawn, puts on his breeches cheerfully, goes out on the race-course and commences running around it at a rate somewhat less than the gait of Eclipse. After having accomplished five, or six, or seven miles, he returns to his house, rouses up his trainers, takes a heavy pair of dumb bells and strikes out some six or seven hundred times to improve his reach and the muscles of his shoulder, striking mostly upward, in consequence of the height of the man with whom he has to contend. He then lays by the dumb bells, and after a few minutes rest, puts on the gloves with one of his trainers, enters into sharp exercise, striking, avoiding, dodging, and wrestling, even to the ground, as in the contingencies of an actual fight.

Mr. Sullivan having thus peppered his trainers, next squares himself before a heavy bag, which hangs pendant from the ceiling by a single cord, and which is stuffed to the weight of his antagonist. Mr. Sullivan deals a mischievous blow at this bag; the bag naturally retires from such an overture, but Mr. Sullivan punches it again, and keeps following it in every direction, as it swings away, until he works himself into a generous perspiration. He then "knocks off," lays by the gloves, and making a thorough wash with cold water, of his arms, chest, neck, and head, adjourns with his two distinguished friends to breakfast.

Mr. Sullivan eats for his breakfast a large beefsteak of the finest cut, and cooked rare, over which he pours a sauce of old English ale, sent to him like the steaks, from the city, and both carefully watched by his trainers, and tasted with as much precaution as the taster of the Sultan would exercise in looking out that his sublime master is not touched with deleterious drug. Sometimes Mr. Sullivan breakfasts on boiled chicken, in which case he usually supervises the excution and preparation of the animal himself.

After breakfast, Mr. Sullivan takes an hour of repose, during which he occupies his time and improves his mind by reading "Boxiana," to keep his imagination fresh in all the different modes of fighting in the prize ring, and fresh in all the various dodges adopted on emergencies, by the most celebrated of the champions of the arena. Having thus refreshed himself, Mr. Sullivan starts out in the open country, bestirs himself actively for some eight or ten miles, in a circuit, and in his travel nurses every acclivity or hollow that offers a chance for novel exercise, as if it were a choice spot in the California Placers. During this exercise Mr. Sullivan is accompanied by his trainers, who occasionally help him in a chase, or stimulate him by vicing in the feat of picking up stones, placed on the ground at equal distances, while on a full run. This is fine exercise, and challenges every nerve and muscle in the body. Mr. Sullivan comes in from this exercise in a warm glow, and while his body is in this state, he

quickly strips all his upper clothing off, and bending downwards, is soused with cold water from his loins down his neck and over his head. This operation is repeated several times, when Mr. Sullivan rises up with a healthful snort, and his trainers fall to on his skin, with coarse towels, which soon leave him of the complexion of a cranberry. Mr. Sullivan then puts on fresh flannel (a daily practice,) and after settling himself in his suspenders, gaily and gracefully invites his two friends to dinner. It being four o'clock, and no other meal being allowed during the day, those gentlemen do not generally refuse. The dinner of Mr. Sullivan is again a fine underdone steak of the largest size, swimming in a sauce of fine old English ale.

After dinner, Mr. Sullivan reposes again, and either whiles away an hour in talking "fight" with his trainers, or in reading "Boxiana," as in the morning. Being refreshed, he takes another sparring bout; another match follows with the dumb bells; when, having his shoulders in play, he wakes up the bag again, and, though it has never done him any harm, and is no way inimical to him except in being of Mr. Hyer's weight, he bangs it viciously and without mercy. Having peppered it to his satisfaction, Mr. Sullivan takes another wash with cold water, when, buttoning himself in his grey overcoat and turning the collar up about his ears, he starts out for a short moonlight or starlight walk of four or five miles on the race course or the road, at the end of which, it being about nine o'clock, he goes to bed.

This is about the day's routine, subject to slight changes as the training advances, and subject also to the substitution of mutton for beef, during the last two or three weeks, immediately preceding the fight.

While all this is going on, Mr. Sullivan lives, in all respects, a virtuous and abstemious life. He will not touch liquor; he will not smoke a cigar; nay, will not stay in a room where one is smoked, and, above all, he does not see Mrs. Sullivan at all—except in a Pickwickian sense. One dereliction of the latter kind would throw him back whole weeks in his training, and put him very low down in the betting. The result is, he is as strong as a lion, as gay as a lark, with a free conscience and a cheerful spirit, and in all respects in that high condition of animal perfection, which enables a man to set at naught all manner of disease or ailment, except perhaps, such as proceed from a hostile collision with some other human machine in as splendid condition as himself. There are those, and their number is thousands, who believe Hyer is the man "to take him down." Out of the thousands on both sides, however, there are none that can positively tell anything about the matter.

It is difficult to conceive a more splendid looking man than Hyer, and we must make full allowance in his favor for those natural advantages of youth, strength, weight, and length of reach, which will tell so tremendously for their possessor, even though pitted against the highest experience and the most superior skill.

The condition of both men is now represented to be very fine, and Hyer is working like Sisyphus to recover a point or two which he lost previous to his exhibition. Both are continually visited by flying detachments of their friends, who having seen them punch away at their bags, and show up their points, leave with a full conviction that their favorite is sure to dispose of his antagonist with as much ease as a fourteen stone M. P. would of an apple woman. On Sunday last, carriage loads went out to Snedicor's and Shaw's, while numerous foot passengers trudged along with sticks and lined the Long Island road, which took them "where they could see Sullivan." Hyer, on the other hand, held a perpetual levee from the morning to the evening of that day, paying the courtesies of reception during the intervals of his exercises. Whatever may happen, they are both in a palmy state of health, and both prepared to bid defiance to the Cholera should it pay a visit to our shores to morrow. In this light, we commend their condition and their virtuous abstemiousness, in every sense, to the serious consideration of the shrivelled and wilted debauchees of the town, and give it as a familiar and tangible evidence to all, whether laity or clergy, of the advantages which necessarily result from cleanliness and exercise.

December 10th.

TRAINING FOR THE FIGHT.

TOM HYER.

We gave last week an account of the mode of training pursued by Yankee Sullivan, preparatory to his forthcoming $10,000 contest with the above named champion in February next, and we now dispose our observations upon Hyer, that both aspects of the matter may be duly estimated, and the friends of both fully aware of the condition of their men.

On Thursday morning last we were called for at our office and plucked from the ocean of our affairs by a distinguished friend connected with the press, aided in his purpose by a couple of bob-tailed ponies, not sent to this country as a present from the Pacha of Egypt. Resistance being out of the question in the face of such an attention, we yielded to Mr. Collins and the ponies, and soon found ourself whirling on the avenue towards M'Comb's dam, being more particularly headed for the inn at that place, kept by Peter Dodge, and entitled the "Romantic Hotel." As we turned into the grounds adjacent to the hotel, we perceived a trio consisting of two very large men and one short one, walking briskly towards us, as if we were trespassers and they were hastening up to challenge our advance. Moreover, one of them, who wore a sort of rough and ready green baize "cutaway," brandished a short cudgel as he stepped along in a manner that did not promise very pleasant entertainment for any who might provoke its applications. A few more revolutions of the wheels, however, and a second look relieved all our concern, and we discovered that the gentleman with the cudgel was no less a person than the Hon. Mr. Hyer, and that the other two with him were his trainers, the tall one being the already somewhat famous George Thompson, or Peter Crawley's sporting "novice," and the short one, the really famous Joe Winrow. We perceived then that the truncheon of Mr. Hyer was not evincive of any belligerent intention, but was only carried and occasionally whirled to supply employment for his animal exuberance, and to keep his upper muscles in continual play.

We received the civilities of recognition from these three distinguished gentlemen with the grace for which we are so celebrated, and then took a brief snap of conversation with Mr. Hyer, in private, as to the state of his health and conscience. But robust and hearty as Mr. Hyer was, he did not on this occasion show to much advantage. A slight and feverish eruption had been thrown out around his mouth two days before, and though it did not impair the appearance of his otherwise fine condition, it disturbed the effect of his handsome features not a little. This harvest had been produced by the reaction of a slight cold, which he had caught upon the sharp physicing he had undergone to get his constitution rapidly in trim for hard work. Waving an adieu, we forbore any further detention of Mr. Hyer from his business, and drove on to the Hotel to await his return, after his exercise. To make this interim the more pleasant, we ordered dinner for ourselves and the ponies, and had the good fortune not only to secure a very pleasant repast, but the felicity of enjoying during the dinner, the conversation of the amiable and lovely hostess of the "Romantic Hotel."

As we expected, our intelligent hostess had her own notions about "this fighting business;" and as it was not, and never is, and never can be, the business of a fighting editor to disagree in opinion with the ladies, and especially with ladies who are amiable and handsome, our hostess had the satisfaction to see us nod a perfect acquiescence to all her observations on "the manly art of self-defence," and to mark, likewise, our perfect agreement with every view she advanced relative to the special match now pending between Mr. Sullivan and Mr. Hyer. While on this por-

tion of our subject, it is due to this worthy lady to say, that she strenuously sets her face against the entire fighting business, in which further view, it will readily be conceived that we agreed with her completely.

Mr. Hyer rises before day break, it appears, being roused by his trainers, and carried away on a brisk walk, to scramble up the beautiful hills, that raise their heads on every side, in and around Bloomingdale, to strive with them in races, not only on the level ground, but up and down the most desperate acclivities. As these three hardy men go about scaling the sharp edges of the mountain side, they look like the Swiss hunters of the Chamois, and many a wondering glance do their strange and hairbreadth exploits draw from the rude workmen who are employed in opening roads and blasting rocks throughout the hilly vicinage.

Having snuffed the fresh air for an hour or more, and exchanged many puffs of hot breath for its invigorating volume, Mr. Hyer returns home by a circuit of some six or seven miles, and devotes himself in striking out with a pair of large dumb-bells, which though heavier than those in use by Sullivan, he handles them with the same facility that a boy would launch an oyster shell quoit or a copper at a hob. Mr. Hyer after having discharged these tremendous slugs at arms' length, some five or six hundred times, takes a short breathing spell, after which he signifies to Mr. Thompson his desire to put on the gloves. The two young giants then confront each other, and commence a sort of spurious warfare, punching each other's heads with muffled blows, and anon, as one pursues the other in advantage, closing in, and tussling to the floor. In these encounters, report says that Mr. Thompson frequently takes the measure of an unmade grave. Eight o'clock having by this time made its appearance on the dial, Mr. Hyer and his two friends adjourn to breakfast where the former confines himself to a very large and very fine steak, broiled slightly over the embers in its natural state, and eat without pepper, salt, or seasoning of any kind. He is allowed no vegetables ; indeed, nothing with this food, but bread, and a very little water, while his less restricted trainers are entitled to discuss the hot coffee, fried potatoes, buckwheat cakes, et cet., which the excellent cook of the establishment knows so well how to get up.

It is here due to those two gentlemen to observe that they do full credit to her preparations, as, from the highest testimony we could gather on the subject, we ascertained that every thing set before them shares the same fate as tow in the mouth of the conjuror, or calves-foot jelly between the jaws of a reporter for the daily press. The same high authority informs us that Mr. Hyer now and then looks wishfully at the other tempting condiments around him, and that on one occasion, despite all the vigilance of Mr. Winrow, who watches him with the fidelity of a cat, he surreptitiously obtained a pinch of salt for his Indian steak, and that on another and more flagrant occasion, he actually stole a turnip. This latter offence was subsequently discovered by Mr. Winrow, and the result was, that Mr. Hyer received a very severe reprimand from that austere disciplinarian.

After breakfast Mr. Hyer reposes, and neither discusses politics or puseyism, nor reads Pilgrim's Progress or Lalla Rookh. Nay, he does not even peruse "Boxiana," as does Mr. Sullivan, but yields to a profound but severe meditation, which no calculations for the battle, or any care of business seems to invade. After an hour has been thus consumed, he is summoned by his trainers to go forth, whereupon the trio start out again and accomplish before dinner a distance of fifteen miles. Hyer coming in the two last on a full run.— In this severe task, the trainers generally save themselves a few miles of the labor by securing command of an eminence, from whence they can supervise their principal in the performance of his work. They very frequently, however, go through the whole task with him, it being desirable that they should enter the ring in tolerable train themselves, in case they should receive a hasty challenge from one of the opposing faction. Mr. Hyer gets in from this fifteen mile trip early enough before 12 o'clock, to enable himself to wash his head and chest and arms with cold water, and to dress with fresh underclothes for dinner. At dinner, which takes place precisely at 12 o'clock, he eats his beef in the same aboriginal style as at breakfast, but moistens his clay on this occasion, by about two wine glasses full of fine Scotch ale. As for Messrs. Winrow and Thompson, they usually perform such feats at this trencher work, as would cover Herr Alexander with confusion, and force magic itself to take a back seat. Hyer on his part disposes of a steak which overhangs the edges of the largest specimen of Devonshire delph, as if it were only a shaving of smoked beef, or a wafer sandwich. The astonished lady who gave us a representation of this department of the training, could not abstain at this portion of the story from raising her hands and solemnly declaring, that the exploits of the trio on these occasions were a "sight to see !" Indeed it seemed to her that they were training "to eat" rather than to fight, and all things considered, we did not wonder at the solemn face and deep concern with which she recounted these deeds of carnivorous prelimination.

After dinner Mr. Hyer again reposes for an hour ; and during this period reflects a little more profoundly even than before. He then takes exercise at the bag, which like the one daily punished by Sullivan, is stuffed to the weight of his antagonist. Mr. Hyer next puts on the gloves with Mr. Winrow, and after a lively sparring bout with that artist, the whole three start out again for another tramp. This excursion commences with easy walking and ends in a run as before. It occupies them until about four o'clock, when in half an hour more Mr. Hyer eats his last meal for the day, and this time, perhaps, contents himself with mutton. The meal closes with the usual rest, after which sparring, the dumb bells, and the bag, wind up the exercises of the day, and eight o'clock finds Mr. Hyer sound upon his virtuous pillow.

The exercises are varied a little from day to day, rowing on the Harlem river being occasionally added to the morning performance, or perhaps thrown in towards the evening.

In all other respects Mr. Hyer, like Mr. Sullivan, lives a perfect chaste and abstemious life, and is a pattern to many who claim to lead up middle aisles, and to sound the key note in sacred psalmistry. In this connexion, it is proper for us to mention that he maintains the same domestic reserve, as does Mr. Sullivan, and would receive Mrs. Hyer, should she visit him at the Romantic Hotel, only with a dignified and Pickwickian courtesy. The reader has now seen the privations, the hardships, and the self-denial which a man must practise before he can arrive at his physical climax, and stand as nature intended him, free from all vitiation of perverted habits. It is a severe, nay, a terrible task, compared with which, the fighting itself is as nothing. Many constitutions break down while undergoing it, while others which are a little worn, dare not attempt the requisite extremes, but come to the score in only half condition. This is not the case, however, with either Hyer or Sullivan. Both have been repeatedly waited upon by curious physicians, who have sounded them in every point and who repeat their examinations with increasing satisfaction, at every advancing stage of the training. With the exception of the trifling eruption which we have noticed as having appeared on Hyer's face, his skin and flesh look fine, and he shows up his points in a truly formidable manner. He is improving fast, and will doubtless continue to do so, if judiciously attended. As he works and perspires away his useless flesh, he does not replace it as do other weary men with copious draughts of water, but eschews everything in the shape of moisture, except what he derives from the juices of his beef, and such slight thimbles full of ale and crystal fluid, as nature absolutely requires. By this system, all the refuse of a long period of case is fast leaving him, and his frame bids fair soon to be reduced to the mere rudiments of muscular strength.

December 16th, 1848.

YANKEE SULLIVAN IN HIS TRAINING.

Some men are born great; some men achieve greatness; and some men have greatness thrust upon them. At least William Shakspeare said so, in the seventeenth century, and we hold him still to be an authority, maugre the theory of the Rev. J. C. Hart, that he was tainted with Jansenism, and was given to whistling through a fork.— "Some men achieve greatness," says the poet, and if an humble descendant of the Timonies may make a comparison not exactly after the fashion of Plutarch, we would venture to point to General Taylor and Yankee Sullivan as striking proofs of the correctness of the proposition. Both of them are great, and both of them have achieved their greatness for themselves. What is more, both of them are fighting men, and though Gen. Taylor might not appear to as much advantage in a twenty-four feet roped ring as Mr. Sullivan, it is equally certain that Mr. Sullivan would not be able to compete with General Taylor in giving the six cuts with a broadsword, or in looking against a battery. Both, however, have overthrown all their adversaries, and are the heroes of every field in which they have ever spread themselves; though the probability is that General Taylor has had the good luck to kill a great many more than Yankee has ever peppered.

As for Sullivan, he seems to be what sporting men, in a spirit of elegant condensation, term an "invince," and succeeds with every thing he undertakes. Whether he will carry his prestige with him after the 7th of February next, depends somewhat upon the consent of Mr. Thomas Hyer, for whom he is now training; but outside, or rather inside of that method of ascertainment, the question of his future fortunes cannot be divined by peeping into a mustard pot. At any rate, and happen what may, Mr. Sullivan cannot be rendered less than a great man, or one of the famous "has beens." while Mr. Hyer, on his side, perils the hope of a great " to come."

When we said that the Hon. Mr. Sullivan was successful in everything he undertook, we had in mind, in addition to the list of his battles, a few recent exploits which he has performed since the commencement of his training, and which are but new proofs of the strong and acute intellect to which he mainly owes all his earlier achievements.

Mr. Sullivan at the commencement of his training bought him a horse, and out of compliment to his friend Country McCleester, for having whipped sixteen Mexicans one afternoon after a very hearty dinner near El Puenta Nacional, he named him " Country."

What were Mr. Sullivan's original contemplations in regard to the animal —whether he intended to spar with him, or to challenge his speed in foot races on the track,—we cannot venture to assert ; but it is a fact, however, which we will put forth, that he so stimulated his nag by the speed of his example, that he has been enabled to get him up to a sufficient rate of velocity to win three matches and pocket the combined stakes of four hundred dollars.

The first of these matches, (all of which were made by Mr. Sullivan in the same off-hand manner in which he would have signed the Declaration of Independence,) was with a somewhat famous trotting nag called " Cambridge Girl," and the stake was $200. This was won by Mr. Sullivan, or by the horse for him—which is the same thing as well in Ireland as in Affghanistan—in two straight heats, the first being performed in 2.44, and the second in 2.46, maugre a heavy vehicle behind him, and a very heavy gentleman inside of it.

The second was with the same antagonist, for $100, and the last with a grey pacer without a name, and which was beaten so badly that it now has no stomach to look a name up.

Thus does Mr. Sullivan amuse himself with incidental " snaps" during his training for his terrifying match, while his hours of more elegant leisure are devoted to the improvement of a large sized bull terrier, which he is ready to

match against the world, and a young brood of game chickens, on which he indulges the most enthusiastic speculations. Every thing that comes under his jurisdiction seems to be improving in condition. Tom O'Donnell, one of his trainers, is in such saucy health that he wishes to redeem the laurels he once lost to Winrow, at a wager of $1000, and Bill Wilson, the other, is willing to fight any thing and every thing that looks like him ; a fruitless hope for manifest reasons in his physiognomy. As for Sullivan, he has reached such a degree of pugnacity and physical power, that some of his friends begin to mistrust the safety of leaving him alone with himself.

Those who wish to see the three above distinguished gentlemen in their most favored positions, may be thoroughly gratified on the evening of Thursday the 21st, at Mager's Concert Hall, in Elizabeth street, where they will all meet in solemn exhibition, similar to the grand convention recently called together by the Hon. Thomas Hyer.— What will render this meeting more exciting, perhaps, is the fact that it immediately precedes the final deposit of the $10,000 stake, and will be probably the last occasion on which the Hon. Mr. Sullivan will " show" before the fight.

December 30, 1848.

SULLIVAN'S LAST EXHIBITION.

According to announcement by yellow placards and otherwise, the grand soiree pugilistic of the Hon. Yankee Sullivan and his trainers came off, or on, according to the taste of the reader, on the night of Thursday the 21st, at the now famous 101 Elizabeth street. Notwithstanding the bitterness of the weather, and the angry driving of the snow, we found assembled at the hour of eight, a very large number of gentlemen in rough pea-coats and seal-skin caps, whose grave countenances and earnest side conversations gave evidence that they were duly impressed with the important nature of the occasion. For our own part, we did not enjoy that elasticity of mind and body which usually characterize our temperament. We had throughout the day been actively engaged in the heavy department of the *Police Gazette*, and it will be easily conceived, even by those very slightly skilled in physics, that an edition of twenty-seven thousand papers carried on our own proper back, from the press-room to the publication office, may disturb the equanimity of the shoulder even of a fighting editor. It was out of the question, therefore, when we arrived, that we should yield to the numerous invitations to spar with Mr. Sullivan, though we find enough vigor left in our five fingers to give him the sign manual, common from the days of Nimrod down, among gentlemen of our order. In consequence of this state of mind and body, we must be excused from giving the reader that particularity of detail which the principal editor usually requires of us on these occasions.

Altogether, the affair was a very superior one of its kind, and though it did not equal in numbers the great mass meeting of the friends of Mr. Hyer, held some weeks ago, the performances of the athletæ who appeared were fully equal to those of the champions who signalized themselves on the former occasion.

*   *   *   *   *   *

The Hon. Mr. Sullivan, and his friend and pitcher, Country McCleester, were finally ushered in the circle, amid the applause of the enthusiastic auditory. It is hardly necessary to relate the friendly pastime which took place between these two gentlemen. Sullivan was dressed in the uniform in which he will meet the Hon. Mr. Hyer on the 7th of February, in order to request him to show cause why judgement should not be entered against him in the matter of $10,000, now pending on the question which of the two have, or will have the handsomest face after that time.

We hardly know how to describe Mr. Sullivan, though it is seldom we are at such a loss in regard to anything in the heavens above, in earth beneath, or in the waters under the earth. It is not enough to say that he is five feet ten, with light legs, deep chest, strong loins, full shoulders, high cheek bones,

muscular neck, quick intelligent eye, and a small flinty looking head, for though all that is true, it will not give a correct idea of his general appearance. At one time he looks like a high trained game cock; next a fighting terrier; again a steam engine in full stroke, and sometimes a flimsy old bag of wool, that would as leaf be beat as not. On the occasion we are now relating, he looked to us more like a hard frost than anything we could think of at the time, and if he had bent his eyes sternly at us during the evening, we should have felt justified in swearing our life against him. It is time for him to look somewhat after this fashion, however, as this is his last appearance before the fight.

On the 10th of January next, or rather in the evening thereof, Mr. Hyer makes his farewell bow to the public at the same place, previous to the event of the 7th of the ensuing month. He is said to be in equally fine condition with his hardy competitor, and his appearance on that occasion will doubtless warrant an equal confidence in his backers, with that which now stimulates the friends of Sullivan.

Let it go as it will, however, a good result has already been effected for the community. The pugilistic spirit has let off the fever for assassination, and the six barrelled pistols and the murderous bowie knives which a few weeks ago were the pet weapons of every rakehell and swash buckler in the town, have given place to the doctrine of the knuckles and hitting from "the shoulder." A peaceful man, may therefore, now walk the street where the fighting crowds perambulate, without fear of being sped to his account by a whiff from some deadly muzzle, or by a slivering stroke from some sweeping blade.

Indeed, so far as this quarrel between Hyer and Sullivan is concerned, we are well convinced that had not the present match been made, the large bands of resolute men who adhere to each, would have met, Philadelphia fashion, before now, and cost the census records some half a dozen lives. In this view, the present fight may be c.u sidered the safety valve of a much greater danger. After the feud is settled, however, all should join to stop such business in the future. We could use cant on this subject if we pleased; but we prefer to talk common sense.

\

January 13th, 1849. ⟩
The 5th month. ⟨

HYER'S LAST EXHIBITION.

The announcement of the last " grand exhibition" of Tom Hyer, drew together, at Mager's Concert Hall, on the night of Wednesday, of last week, a company ranging between seven hundred and a thousand people, who, at a dollar a head, seemed to afford the most profound satisfaction to the Hon. Mr. Hyer, as he stood in a position of dignified reflection near the head of the stairs, in the first smile of the evening. Surrounding Mr. Hyer were several amateurs and " Past Grands" in the fistic art, gazing in admiration at the " Royal Arch" before them, and occasionally making side whispers to their friends, by way of evincing their high estimation of his qualities and condition. A nod from the Hon. Mr. Hyer, to any new comer, under these circumstances, was a compliment of no ordinary magnitude; so when the circle of reverent outsiders saw him spit in his hand at our approach, and give us a grasp similar to that to be exchanged between Mayor Havemeyer and General Taylor, when the latter visits the city, a singular expression of envy might be seen in the faces of all surrounding lookers on. The Hon. Mr. Hyer has a great power of grip, and right well do the five fingers of our right hand recollect it.

The Hon. Mr. Hyer looked in superb condition, and fully justified the high en encomiums that were passed upon him. He stood his full six feet two and a half; his frame seemed reduced to its most nervous measure, and the ruddy hardness of his features showed a glow of tough and vigorous health, that could hardly be exceeded in animal condition. In attire and outline, he was, perhaps, the best dressed and handsomest man present; and when we say this we give

full consideration to the claims and pretensions of all the mustachioed exquisites, pugilistic competitors, dandy policemen, editors and lawyers of a high and low degree, who account themselves " some" in the vocabulary of good looks, and who were then and there " on hand."

The great feature of the evening now arrived, and amidst a strong sensation and general applause, the Hon. Mr. Hyer and Mr. Thompson leaped upon the stage. In standing up in his silk net shirt, Hyer looked more gaunt than we expected, and his shoulder blades showed as sharp through the glossy woof, as the ribs of a racer through a chestnut hide. He is certainly under the mark of one hundred and seventy-five, while Thompson, on the other hand, has fattened with his exercise, and showed to the extent of some two hundred weight.

As soon as the combatants had bowed to the audience with the grace of Barnum's giant, and touched the tips of each other's gloves with dignified courtesy, they squared away amid a profound silence, which evinced the deep interest of the audience in what was about to take place. Hyer did not hold himself so stiff as at his former exhibition, though he still leaned back more than satisfied the opinions of the judicious. His design seems to be to hold his face from danger in the coming fight, which is very well, if he can at the same time protect his lower ribs. One of these two points, however, he must yield to his acute antagonist, and it is a matter of considerable question among the learned in pugilistic science, which of the two relinquishments will subject him to the lightest injury. Apart from its disfigurements, the face is the safest point to give away, so far as ultimate results upon the health are to be considered, while the blows upon the body, though they leave the mind clear and permit a longer struggle, are more lasting and hurtful in their effects. It is the difference between champagne, which whizzes the thoughts beyond command and soon lays its victim underneath the table, and blazing alcohol, which bites into the bowels and leaves a permanent imprint upon the inner system. Hyer seems to have chosen to preserve his features, but while he holds his head well up, he has at the same time adopted a firm lower guard, which would be very difficult for any man to pass, except, perhaps, the Hon. Mr. Sullivan.

The first round or two between Mr. Hyer and his friend was rather prosy in its method, consisting mostly of a few feints, and a cautious pantomime, in the course of which but two or three good hits were made by Hyer, without any earnest disposition, as it seemed to us, on the part of Mr. Thompson, to return them. Indeed, he seemed to satisfy himself with keeping on his guard, and when he did return, his blows were handsomely, or, to use perhaps a more correct term, *showily*, stopped. Five or six rounds more followed, of much the same character as the first, but during the whole the surprise of all who knew Thompson's qualities was great in the extreme; that he did not display to better advantage. The backers of the beneficiary, however, insisted that the cause of this, was Thompson's dread of Hyer's counter-hits; while others of the same class, who pretended to be deeper into the secret, gave several profound winks, and slyly indicated that Mr. Sullivan's friends " were not a going to learn any pints from that are set-to." However this may be, the encounter might very properly be termed a " wooden " one. Had they been a pair of automatons arranged on mechanical principles, and pulled to a set method by a string, they could not have deserved less independent credit. It is certain that the affair did not give very general satisfaction, and the opinion of the audience seemed to be, that both the parties might have done much better, had they pleased.

The whole affair was interesting, however, as the grand precursor of the fight; and the satisfaction of seeing, in action, a man who is soon desperately to contend for the enormous stake of $10,000, was worth the individual outlay at the door.

There will be no more exhibitions previous to the actual contest, and each man will be as busy as possible in making the final preparations for the struggle.

As for Sullivan, having won the choice of ground, he is now on his journey, via. Philadelphia, to select it. He will make the most of his advantage by scraping acquaintance with every individual for five miles round the country in which the ring is to be pitched, and thus will secure a local feeling in his favor in advance of this antagonist, that will protect his interests, if necessary, on the ground. His journey is, therefore, a sort of electioneering expedition; and he will also make it one of profit, by giving an exhibition in Philadelphia, and perhaps in Baltimore, during his advance or his return. These chances the Hon. Mr. Hyer is deprived of, not being entitled to know the location of the arena until within ten days of the fight. It is said, however, that he is cheerfully content with this disadvantage, having perfect confidence in his ability, under all circumstances, to take care of the end of the chapter. As to this, we shall see.

Where the Hon. Mr. Sullivan will pitch his stakes is not yet within conjecture, though many hope he will choose the District of Columbia, so that Congress may adjourn, after the fashion of Parliament, for the Epsom races, to see this most absorbing event since the Presidential election, or the outbreak of the California fever.

THE GREAT PRIZE FIGHT,

BETWEEN

Tom Hyer and Yankee Sullivan,

FOR TEN THOUSAND DOLLARS.

WON BY HYER IN SEVENTEEN MINUTES AND EIGHTEEN SECONDS.

From the N. Y. Police Gazette of Feb. 10, 1849.

The great prize fight, which has been the standard topic of conversation for the last six months in fighting circles, and which, to confess the truth, has occupied a large share of the attention of refined society during the same period of time, came off, according to agreement, on Wednesday, the 7th inst., at

Rock Point, mouth of Still Pond Creek, in Kent county, on the Eastern shore of Maryland, about 40 miles from Baltimore.

The location originally intended for the arena, was Pool Island, in the upper part of Chesapeake bay, which had been selected by Sullivan three weeks before as the most eligible spot for the intended meeting, as he had heard that its jurisdiction was disputed, or divided by the State of Maryland and the Government of the United States. Moreover, it was thirty miles away, with but two buildings, except the lighthouse stationed on it, and therefore could not produce much local interference with the proceedings of the invading hordes who would pour upon it on the indicated day, as if from the mouth of the everlasting pit.

But while Pool Island lay perfectly quiet, showing no signs of disgust or opposition, obstacles were breeding in Baltimore, and by-and-by that virtuous city, which usually has a man a week killed in its streets, or two or three riots in the same period of time, became so indignant at the idea of making a hundred thousand dollars or so, by having a match of fisticuffs within electric distance of its borders, that it organized voluntary patrols to frown down the outrage, and stuffed a broken winded steamboat with crowds of infantry armed to the teeth, to rake the Chesapeake up and down, and in default of capturing the combatants, to sing Watts's hymns in honor of Gov. Thomas, the night through.

These preparations on the part of the authorities of the State of Maryland, and of the city of Baltimore, to stop the fight, commenced on Tuesday morning, and both the steamboats which had been chartered by the several crowds, were paralysed by the authorities with writs against their captains, and one of them, the Boston, was chartered by the State for the pursuit. While things were in this condition, Hyer, apprehending, and correctly as it proved, that warrants would be despatched after him and his trainers slipped away from his training ground and went to Carroll's Island, a little island next to Pool's. Sullivan had anticipated him in this prudent course, having arrived at Carroll's Island on Monday afternoon, and crossed to Pool's before Hyer's arrival. Hyer shortly after crossed to Pool Island also, and put up at the house attached to the light-honse, while Sullivan had secured the only other place for human accommodation, at some distance off.

Leaving the principal parties thus bestowed, we will now return to Baltimore, to see how matters progress with those who have charge of the grand preliminaries of the affair, and with those likewise who were endeavoring to get a thimbleful of reputation out of the excitement, by trying to stop it.

Late in the afternoon of Tuesday, the backers, judges, referee, bottle-holders, &c., of both parties, in Baltimore, finding that there was to be no steamboating on the following morning, hired two oyster smacks, and embarked, to the number of one hundred, each side, and at 10 o'clock, put out upon the Chesapeake, in a bright cold night, but so tempestuous with the wind, that the captains of the pungees had some ugly doubts themselves as to the safety of the surface of the bay.

The name of the boat containing Sullivan's party was the "Whig," and as she swung from the dock, the Boston was "firing up" to carry her military cargo to the same place to intercept them. However, the smacks sailed away unmolested. At the same hour, High Constable Gifford, of Baltimore, left with thirteen men, across the land to the nearest point opposite the designated scene of combat. At a quarter before 12, the Boston got off on her errand We have now three expeditions all directed to one spot, two of which were in pursuit, and the third dodging the chase.

.THE DESCENT OF THE POLICE.

The pungees arrived at the island first; the "Whig" reaching the shore at half-past one, p. m. Joe Beard, of Baltimore, and Country McCleester were then sent ashore to see if Sullivan was on the island, receiving directions, if he were asleep. not to wake him, but to let him have his natural rest till five o'clock. They were then to wake him and tell him the steamboat was coming and to hurry him on board. Following these directions, Joe, finding Sullivan asleep, sat down by the fire as a sentry and went to sleep himself. Hyer's boat had now arrived, when a similar course was pursued in relation to him, the two boats meanwhile swinging to their anchors, and waiting for the daylight and the embarkment of their men.

In the meantime, Captain Gifford and his thirteen arrived upon the western beach of the bay at three o'clock, and seizing a boat in the name of the State, they unmoored, and set out in the biting atmosphere for the island. As they approached it, they perceived the steamer Boston entering on the scene. They passed under her bows and hailed her, but such was the howling of the wind and the coldness of the night, that they were unheard. Gifford then debarked, and with his force, proceeded to Hyer's house.

HYER'S ESCAPE.

The friends of Hyer were not keeping a bright look-out; but one of them, nevertheless, heard the tramp of the police and ran up stairs in time to give Tom notice, whereupon he jumped up instantly and putting Thompson, his trainer, in his bed, ran down stairs, and crept under the cot of a negress on the ground floor.

While thus surrounded, Dutch Charley conveyed him his clothes, and he commenced dressing with the utmost rapidity, to take advantage of the first opportunity of escape. At this moment the officers were being led up stairs by the owner of the house, who knew nothing of the metamorphosis that had taken place. The owner of the house pointed to Thompson in the bed. Seeing that he was a huge man, and taking him for Hyer, the officers soon desisted from their attempts to pull the cover from their attempts to pull the cover from his face, and leaving a small detachment in charge, set out with the rest for Sullivan's house. As soon as they had gone, Hyer broke through the sash of the room below, and commenced

running towards the beach, but he was hailed by Winrow from a tree, who joined him in the flight. Arriving at the beach, they found two men with a boat belonging to the steam propellor "Columbia," from Philadelphia, which had just arrived off the island with about one hundred passengers, to see the fight. They thus reached their schooner, and were safe.

SULLIVAN'S ESCAPE.

When the police arrived at Sullivan's house, after leaving Hyer's, Joe Beard was dozing by the fire, but not so sound as not to hear Gifford ask a question, and the man of the house reply, that Sullivan was up stairs. He gave the alarm in time, and Sullivan sprang out of the window, but being confronted with two men, one of whom levelled a pistol at him, was glad to retire back. He then roused Tom O'Donnell, his second, from his sleep, and with that quickness of thought for which he always has been remarkable, threw a cloak over Tom O'Donnell's shoulders, and clapping his hands, exclaimed, "Run, Sullivan, run, as if hell had kicked you!" The officers, completely deceived at this, seized O'Donnell, while the real Simon Pure slipped away. Sullivan then ran to a tree and climbed it for a few moments in case they should return, but seeing they did not, he slipped down, and crawling low into the advancing dawn, made for the beach like his opponent. Meantime the officers were lugging O'Donnell along, while Gifford would renew his grip on his collar every minute, like a man who doubted he was in a dream of fortune, and exclaim at intervals in half soliloquy, "Ah, Sullivan, you're pretty smart, but you're not smart enough for us!" What he said when he discovered how Sullivan had fooled him, we have not heard. At the beach Sullivan was met by Johnny McGrath, the ex-champion of the English light-weights, who taking him on his shoulders, marched with him through the surf, and placed him in the propeller's boat, and had him rowed on board.

THE EMBARKATION.

Soon after this the Cumberland moved

towards Sullivan's pungee and put him aboard. The propeller then started up the bay, and the Boston, with the military, mistaking her motions, supposed the two men had been taken on board of her and were going off to tight. The latter, therefore, set out in chase, leaving the two pungees, which really contained the objects of their search, behind. Sullivan's boat then hailed Hyer's, and Colton, to guard against surprise in case they should leave the island and Hyer's party remain on the ground, and win by being present merely, called out, "Show us Hyer and we'll show you Sullivan." Hyer and Sullivan were then brought up. As soon as they gazed upon each other, the eyes of the latter flashed like fire, and he shook his fist at his tall opponent with a passionate epithet. " Look here, my little man, " said the captain of the " Whig, " "if you allow yourself to get in such a passion on the start, you'll get whipped. " " Will you follow us ? " said Beckett, Sullivan's principal backer, to the opposing judge. "Yes," said Hyer, answering himself, "follow you anywhere." They then bore up the Chesapeake, finishing up the picture of the chase, the propeller being ahead, in the distance, the Boston next, and the two pungees, which were taken for outsiders going to see the fight, coming last. After Sullivan's schooner had got two or three miles away, those who were on board of her were surprised to find they were not followed by the other pungee, when dreading a ruse of Hyer's party again, they returned. But when they got back they found their suspicions were unjust, and that Hyer's pungee was aground. Sullivan took the opportunity to send ashore for his fighting shoes which he had left behind, in his flight.

Time kept running away, and still Hyer's boat stuck fast, and in the chagrin of delay the eager parties were more than once tempted to take advantage of the absence of their pursuers and the readiness of the ring, which stood " all set" before their eyes, to settle the business of the day before they got back. Had they known how little time it was to take they might have done so

with ease. Meantime, the Boston had discovered her error, and was returning fast. By good luck for the fighters, however, Hyer's schooner got afloat just as she came up, and by bad luck for the hungry sogers the Boston got aground at the same time, and the two pungees, free at last, sailed off together, with their fingers to their bowsprits, in derision at the ineffectual attempts of all Baltimore and Maryland to interfere with the boys of New York.

It was now settled that Hyer's boat should take the lead, and all hands being rather wolfish by their numerous disappointments, agreed to drop upon the first conveinent spot, whether it was in Maryland, or Delaware, or Virginia, or hell. At half-past one o'clock they espied four or five small oyster smacks, and judging it to be a proper place, the crowd, to the number of some two hundred, debarked.

THE DEBARKATION.

The motley crowd, glad to set foot on shore after the lengthened cramp which they had undergone in their close quarters, hastily poured out, and swarmed in little buzzing knots upon the shore. Sullivan was among the first who felt the terra firma which he was to make such familiar acquaintance with before the afternoon was out, and espying a house at the distance of some three quarters of a mile ahead, set out to reach it before the opposing party, in order to secure what advantage there might be in the earliest acquaintance with the inmates. Hyer, more prudent, however preferred to avoid the trudging through the snow, and laid himself down in the bottom of a cart stuffed half full of straw, and suffered himself to be driven easily to the same place. A mile of circuit, which might have been shortened by another path, brought them to the dwelling on the beach, and under its roof both the combatants found equal shelter. Each took up his quarters in large rooms on either side of the main hall, and huge fires of crackling hickory soon streamed up the capacious chimney-pieces, either in honor of the unexpected comers, or in deference to their powers of annoyance, should they ne treated with any less difference than was due to the actual lords in fee simple and manorial right, to the estate.

The principals, both in good spirits, took their seats by the cheerful fires, while their satellites in reverential silence, grouped themselves around to listen to the least expression which might fall from those who were to be the heroes of the day.

SETTING THE STAKES.

Meanwhile the more interested of the attaches of the separate sides, occupied themselves in making preparations for the ring. The spot selected for the arena by Sullivan's friends was between the house and the farm, and the location was considered favorable to the former, from the lumpy character of the surface, as it was expected that his wrestling qualities would enable him to throw his heavier antagonist, and punish him the more severely by the sharpness of his falls. The friends of Hyer seemed, however, to have a due appreciation of the policy of this intention, for after the snow was shovelled from the surface they spaded fresh earth and sprinkled the entire platform of the ring, so that it was made as soft and elastic as a carpet. The stakes were then procured from pine billets found in the neighborhood, and for want of better gear, the top gallant halyards of the "Whig" were taken for the ropes. In the haste of their operations, the ring was not set exactly square, but had an oblique twist towards the sun, while the southern side presented a slight acclivity which promised, when it was caught by interested and observant eyes, to become the bitterest battle ground. At ten minutes past four everything was set, and notice was given to the parties in the house that all was ready.

IN THE RING.

Sullivan, shortly after this summons, emerged from the house, being preceded by one of his seconds who carried a pair of hot bricks, which were intended for his feet while waiting for the signal to begin. As he approached the ring his appearance was hailed with cheers,

and when he threw in his cap, which was a velvet one of a rich dark green, the most enthusiastic shouts were heard from his friends. He took his seat upon a chair that was provided for him, and with his feet upon the bricks, waited for the entrance of his foe. In two or three minutes more, Hyer came forth, borne on the brawny shoulders of his friend Dutch Charley, and as he neared the ropes, he shyed his castor, a foggy looking piece of felt, into the arena before him. Another burst of clamor then rent the sky, and amid increased enthusiasm, each man tied his colors to the stake. That of Hyer was the spangled ensign of his country, while Sullivan's was a green fogle with oval spots of white. Both men sat down on their seconds' knees, and confronted each other while the final preliminaries were arranged.

While thus awaiting the summons to the ordeal, the seconds, Joe Winrow and John Ling, the first for Hyer and the latter for Sullivan, came forward and made the toss for choice of ground. This was won for Sullivan, who, thereupon, reserved the corner where he already sat, giving to his antagonist the bright and dazzling sun directly in his eyes. The seconds now took their corners, Tom Burns taking the place of the captured Thompson, Hyer's regular trainer, and Country McCleester supplying the absence of Tom O'Donnell, on the part of Sullivan. Outside the ropes, in waiting on the latter, was Stephen Wilson, acting as a bottle-holder, and on the other corner, similarly affixed, was the brother of the lofty champion. At twenty minutes past four exactly, Winrow asked the question, "Are you ready?" "Yes," said Sullivan, rising and beginning to strip off his outer clothes, an operation in which he was immediately followed by Hyer, and which was accomplished by both with the celerity of a stage metamorphosis. In less than a minute they stood stripped to the waist, and attired in their neat fighting clothes. Such was the absorbing interest which held possession of all minds during these proceedings, that but a single bet was offered and made. Indeed, $35 was the entire amount that was wagered on the ground, and ·this was bet even.

THE MEN.

As the antagonists stood up, all ready for the strife, there was a marked disparity in the appearance of the men. Hyer stood six feet two and a half inches, and Sullivan but five feet ten and a half. The weight of the former, moreover, was in the close neighborhood of 185, while the avoirdupois of Sullivan was rated no higher than 155, making a difference of thirty pounds in Hyer's favor. As to condition, both seemed equal. They were as finely developed in every muscle as their physical capacity could reach, and the bounding confidence which sparkled fiercely in their eyes, showed that their spirits and courage were at their highest mark. Sullivan, with his round compact chest, formidable head, shelving flinty brows, fierce glaring eyes, and clean-turned shoulders, looked the very incarnation of the spirit of mischievous genius; while Hyer, with his broad, formidable chest, and long muscular limbs, seemed as if he could almost trample him out of life, at will.

THE FIGHT.

Before coming to the scratch, the umpire for Sullivan asked the seconds of his side if they intended to examine Hyer's shoes, but they declined the formality as a matter of but little consequence, upon which the word was given and the men came up. According to rule they were obliged to shake hands before they began, but they performed this ceremony warily and at extreme arm's length. It was the business of the seconds next to do the same, but before they could reach the scratch to go through the idle ceremony, the eager crowd shouted them back, and they gave way at once to the gladiatorial show.

Round 1st.—Sullivan with his arms well up and every muscle swelling with its preparation, darted towards Hyer, who stood resolutely waiting for him with his body well forward and in formidable readiness: and coming up to him with a sort of run, let fly with his left at Hyer's head, but did not get it in; he then got away from a short attempt of Hyer to counter with his left, but Hyer followed the effort with an instant discharge of his right in Sullivan's forehead, which made a long abrasion of the scalp, but which, notwithstanding the power of the blow, showed neither blood nor discoloration at the time. Gathering himself for a return, Sullivan then rushed in at the body, and after two or three ineffective exchanges clinched his antagonist with the underhold and struggled for the throw. This was the great point on which was to depend the result of the fight. Sullivan relied mainly for success upon his superior wrestling, and it was calculated by his friends and backers, that a few of his favorite cross-buttocks would break his young antagonist in his lithe and graceful waist, and not only render him limpsey with weakness, but stun him with the falls. The most terrible anxiety therefore existed as to the result of this endeavor. In its fierce agitations, the spectators, who stood in an outer ring of plank laid over the snow some feet distance from the ropes of the arena, involuntarily rushed forward and swarmed against the ropes. Two or three times did Sullivan knot his muscles with an almost superhuman effort, but all served only to postpone his overthrow; for when he had spent his power by these terrible impulsions, his iron adversary wrenched him to the ground with the upper hold, and fell heavily, prone upon his body. This decided the largest part of the outside betting in favor of the upper man, and shouts of the most terrific joy went up for Hyer. The depression of Sullivan's friends was equal in degree, and they began to get an inkling that they had underrated their opponent.

Round 2d.—As soon as time was called, both men hurried to the scratch, Hyer working to the upper slope of the ring, where stood the judges and the referee, and thus slanting the sun between his body and that of his opponent, instead of taking its beams directly in his eyes. As Sullivan came up this time, the blood from the scratch upon his forehead made crimson confession of its severity, and elated the friends of the tall one with shrieks of "first blood for Hyer!" Sullivan at this hosanna rushed desperately in, and meeting Hyer where he paused to receive his charge, delivered a heavy blow with his right on Hyer's left eye, taking a counter on his opposing ogle in return. Sullivan kept close up, and both kept striking with the rapidity of two cocks as they fly together, rendering it almost impossible to see where, or how, the hits were discharged. It was evident, however, that the rally had not been attended with serious effect to either side. A feint from Sullivan, and a dodge from Hyer, intervened; when another rally followed, Sullivan taking in return for a couple of body blows two severe discharges on the left eye, by a sort of half upper cut with the right hand, which brought the blood again. Sullivan then rushed in and clinched; he caught the underhold again, but his efforts were naught, and he was twisted to the ground as if he had been a man of grass, his huge antagonist falling upon him as before with his entire weight. Shouts for Hyer.

Round 3d.—The hopes of Yankee's friends were now fading fast, and indeed he seemed impressed himself with the idea that he was overmatched. He looked at his opponent with a sort of wild astonishment as he came up, but with a desperate courage, as if conscious nothing but the most reckless policy alone could help him, he rushed up to the scratch, and gathering cautiously, after a wicked pause, he softened his apparent intention with a feint, but finding Hyer would not be drawn out, he let fly right and left, and catching Hyer with the latter blow upon the body (some say the neck) staggered him backwards a couple of steps and brought him to a sitting position on the ground. The shouts now went up on Sullivan's side, and amidst the uproarious glee he went smiling to his corner.

Round 4th —Both came up this time with the utmost alacrity, Sullivan encouraged by his success, and Hyer showing the utmost eagerness to get even. Sullivan hurried up, and led off without getting in, and Hyer, in his ex-

citement, not only returned short, but open handed. This excited the attention of the former's backer, who, while on the point of crying out, "Now, you've got him, Jim," discovered that Sullivan was open handed too. The warning, however, brought both of them to their senses, and made them close their fists. Hyer then hit out right and left, executing with the latter on the old spot and taking a body blow in return. Sullivan then ran in and clinched, but his hold did him no good, for he was thrown in the same manner as before, Hyer falling on him and lying across him for several seconds, until his henchmen could come slowly and take him off. Expressions of dissatisfaction here broke out from Sullivan's friends, and the umpire of that side claimed "foul," on the score that the upper man was not sooner removed. The question was put to the referee, who, however, decided "fair."

Round 5th.—Sullivan, who had suffered considerably in the last round by his eagerness to improve the advantage he had gained in the third, led off with the same reckless spirit and with the same desperate aim. He struck wildly right and left at the head, but getting stopped, next tried the body. His incautiousness, however, received a heavy punishment in the shape of a tremendous right-hand paixhan on the left eye, which hit him down upon his hand, with one knee touching the ground. Hyer rushed forward to hit again, but checking himself, he raised his hands as if afraid of being tempted to a foul blow, and moving backwards, turned towards his corner. At this moment Sullivan's umpire, supposing the round at an end, dropped his eye to his watch and started his time. It happened, however, that as Hyer had turned away, Sullivan, apparently wild, had risen and recommenced the round; whereupon Hyer turned upon him and pressed him by main strength to the ground. While this supplementary struggle was going on, the umpire raised his eyes, and supposing Hyer had turned to attack Sullivan after the round had finished, as he had marked it, called out "foul." The character of the renewal was explained to him, however, whereupon he withdrew his complaint.

Round 6th.—Sullivan now began to show his punishment and fatigue in a slight nervousness of his legs, but still he ran boldly up for desperate fighting, as game as a pebble, and as resolute as if the battle was still within his reach. Several rapid exchanges were then made, Sullivan catching it on the right eye brow, in a counter to a body hit. Hyer then fought Sullivan to the ropes, and bent him backwards over them. Some sharp fibbing took place, which, proving rather unpleasent to Hyer, he seized Sullivan and threw him and fell on him, with his arm across his neck. He remained in this position for some moments, without interference by his seconds, who saw that it was to his. advantage, whereupon a claim of "foul" was made by Sullivan's judge. The Referee, however, decided "fair."

It was likewise claimed that in rising Hyer had pressed improperly on Sullivan's neck, but the claim was not made out.

Round 7th.—Sullivan, breathing short, and exhibiting much fatigue, came up the same as ever, and Hyer, as before, stood on the slope to forbid his passage one inch upon his ground. The little man, as he approached his huge antagonist, seemed as if dispirited by the decision of the referee, while he was nearly spent with the severe exertions that he had made to hit and get away. But he hit with no effect, while the blows of his powerful antagonist made the blood flow profusely down his face, although they had really less effect upon the unfortunate left eye than it seemed. Several exchanges were made, all against Sullivan, when he rushed in again at his wrestling hold, and found the ground as he had done in these close encounters every time before.

Round 8th.—The hit in the eye which Hyer received in the second round, now showed its colors, and puffed up with dirty pride and vanity over the surrounding flesh. Sullivan's left eye was no better; indeed worse, and bore many testimonials in crimson cre-

vices of Hyer's black and long knuckles. Sullivan again made play from the jump, but got nothing in. As he hit out at the body, Hyer struck short with the left, as was his custom every time, when he meditated mischief with his right hand, and then let go with his dexter mawley, driving the blood out from the left eye in gory spray, but still not knocking his staunch opponent down. Sullivan finding that he could not parry off these terrific hits, ran in again, but was thrown as before, Hyer falling on him, and lying with his breast across Sullivan's chest, neck, and face. Hyer's seconds were again slow in coming up to take him off, upon which another appeal of "foul" was made to the referee, who, however, decided "fair," though he admitted he could not see at all times, in consequence of the crowd getting between him and the men, and jostling him about since the first round.

Round 9th.—"Time" came round quick at this "call," as much of the thirty seconds was consumed while the men were on the ground. Both men came up bloody to the scratch; Sullivan being literally clotted with gore, while the clear crimson smoked on Hyer's chest, from a lance wound which had been made under his right eye to prevent it from closing out his sight. He was also dabbled with the drains which ran from Sullivan, and which painted his arms and bosom every time they closed. Sullivan walked up to the scratch this time with a freshened vigor, and showed the same determination as when he commenced the battle. Hyer, who was cool, and apparently unfatigued, at once saw the real condition of his man, and concluding that it was now time to change his tactics, led off for the first time. The Yankee seemed better capable of resisting this mode of warfare than making a successful aggression, and dodged two wicked looking blows; but in endeavoring to return with a rush, he brought Hyer to his usual defensive position. He then took Sullivan's blows without wincing or endeavoring to stop them, being satisfied to take advantage of the right hand counter which from the first had told with such terrible effect. Sullivan rushed in again to save himself from punishment, and was thrown, with Hyer on him.

Round 10th.—Sullivan came up with his hands open and showing distress. He led off with ineffectual passes, which only served to provoke punishment, and give him the return of a wicked right-handed hit in the old place, which staggered him to the ground.

Round 11th.—Hyer, strong on his pins, respiring regularly, and evidently in possession of all his strength. He waited for Sullivan as before, and though Yankee came up rather slower than before, Hyer was content to wait his approach rather than alter a method by which he was getting on so well. On meeting at the scratch, a few rapid hits were made, which ended in a clinch and a wrestle to the ground, Hyer uppermost as before, but with Sullivan's leg locked over his until he was taken off.

Round 12th.—This time both men came up quick, and Sullivan led off, hitting wildly and madly right and left, while his cool antagonist, watching his chance, took a short hit for the privilege of countering on the old spot. Sullivan then rallying his energies, tried the Secor dodge, and endeavored to slip under Hyer's right arm, to hit him from behind, but he was stopped and caught by Hyer with the left, on the top of the head, with a round blow, which discharged him to the ground.

Round 13th.—Up to this time all the fighting was done in Sullivan's corner, making Hyer's boast good that he should not have an inch more than twelve feet to do his fighting in. This round commenced by sharp exchanges right and left, as if they had come together for the first time. At length Hyer, finding it was all his own way, rallied Sullivan sharply, and driving him to the ropes, backed him over them, and entered into a smart exchange of fibbing. Hyer caught hold of the ropes while thus engaged, when a man from Boston, by the name of Hennessy, seized his thumb, and bent it backwards from its hold, whereupon Hyer let go, and clinching

Sullivan, wrenched him to the ground and fell upon him.

Round 14th.—Sullivan giving out fast; Hyer perceiving it entered briskly on the offensive, fought him to the ropes and fibbed him on them as before. After an exchange of this kind of work, Hyer jerked him from the ropes, and clinching, wrestled him to the ground and fell upon him.

Round 15th.—Sullivan shaky on his pins, and Hyer apparently as strong as ever. As Sullivan came up and attempted to hit out, he slipped; Hyer rallied him to the ropes, hitting him right and left in the pursuit, and bending him again over the ropes. During this struggle he caught his arm, and bending it backward in its socket, gave it a wrench that must have caused the most agonizing pain; he then clinched and threw him to the ground and fell upon him as before.

Round 16th.—When time was called, Sullivan was slow in rising from his second's knee, and it was evident that his fighting star had set, for the day at least. He walked in a limpsey manner towards the score, but when he put up his left arm the tremor which shook it showed that it was distressed by pain. Hyer did not wait for him, but advancing beyond the score, let fly both right and left in Sullivan's face, who, though he could not return it, took it without wincing in the least. Hyer then rushed him to the ropes again, and after a short struggle there, threw him and fell heavily upon him, in which position Sullivan locked his leg over him again, as if he would hold him in his place. When he was taken off, Sullivan was found to be entirely exhausted, and when lifted up reeled half round and staggered backward towards the ropes. The fight was done. He could not come in again, and one of his seconds took him from the ring, without waiting for time to be called. Hyer's second, as soon as this took place, advanced to take Sullivan's colors as their trophy, but being interfered with and denied by Ling, Hyer rushed forward himself, and seizing Ling by the arm, enabled his friend to take the prize. The shouts then went up for the victor, and the party commenced unthreading the stakes of their halyards, for the voyage back.

Thus ended a contest which has excited more interest than any other pugilistic encounter that ever took place in this country ; but which, though it engaged thousands of minds for a period of six long months, was done up, when, once begun, in seventeen minutes and eighteen seconds.

The boats soon got up sail after the battle was over, and made for Pool Island again on their return. On arriving at that place they found the steamer Boston still aground, and as her warlike freight came crowding to the side, the pungees gave them three times three as a compensation for the disappointment they had received, in neither arresting the principals, nor in getting a peep at the fight.

CERTIFICATE OF THE JUDGES.

We hereby certify, that we have seen the above rounds in manuscript as prepared for publication in the National Police Gazette, and believe they present as full, correct, and impartial a report of the fight which they describe, as could be made under the circumstances.

H. COLTON,
J. J. WAY.

REMARKS.

The foregoing contest may be aptly termed a " hurricane fight." From the commencement to the close it was bitter, unremitting, and determined. On the part of Sullivan it consisted of a series of quick and almost superhuman efforts to outfight and stun his antagonist from the start, while Hyer, who seemed to be thoroughly aware of his intent, contented himself with standing at the scratch and forbidding any entrance to his side, by the tremendous counter hits which he delivered in return for Sullivan's rapid visitations. He did not attempt to make parrying a leading feature of his policy, but for the greater portion of the time cheerfully met Sullivan's blows for the chance of countering back. He had evidently settled upon this as his policy for the fight, judging correctly, that if

hit and hit was to be the order of the day, the weakest structure must go to pieces in the struggle. In addition to this, Hyer showed excellent skill in fighting, and his method of hitting short with the left, as a preliminary to the paixhan discharge of the right, in the style of a half upper cut, could not have been excelled in the use which he made of it, by the best hitters who have ever shown themselves in the prize ring. To help him still further, he was cool and self-possessed, with the exception of a moment or two at the opening of the fourth round, when he seemed either shaken by his fall, or stung from his control, by the cheers which greeted Sullivan for the handsome blow. Sullivan on the other hand fought wild and over eager. He did not display that shrewdness and care which has characterized all his previous fights, but seemed to consider himself in the ring, not so much to decide some three hundred thousand dollars, as to revenge upon Hyer, in the bitterest and most sudden manner, the personal hatred that stood between them. He hurried to the scratch at every round, and commenced leading off right and left, and when obliged to take it more severely than he bargained for, invariably rushed in for a clinch, notwithstanding each succeeding round proved more conclusively than those which had gone before, he could not throw his man, and that these reverses invariably brought upon him the severest punishment of all. He was twisted to the ground invariably by the superior strength of his antagonist, and what in view of this, was surprising to his friends, he would resist strongly every time, instead of slipping down as easily as possible to save his strength. As to Hyer's lying on him to the extent he did, there has been much dispute and while one party claims it to have been " foul," the other insists that it was a pardonable advantage. Between these two opinions the referee decided "fair." He decided so, properly. There is no rule in " Fistiana" which prescribes the length of time which a man may be allowed to lie upon another between the rounds, but the common law of the ring gives to each side the possession of their man, the instant the round is ended. Sullivan was, therefore, the property of his seconds the instant he touched the ground, and they were entitled to him, though obliged to throw twenty men from his body to get at him. It was natural for Hyer's seconds to let him lie when he had the advantage, but it was the duty of Sullivan's seconds to insist upon their rights, and to acquaint the other side that, if they did not take their man off in time, they would throw him off. This they had a right to do, and the result of their not having done it, was, that while Hyer, after the struggle and the throw, would repose at ease on Sullivan's body and draw respirations of fresh atmosphere, Sullivan was crushed with the incumbent weight, and capable of catching only a few muffled breaths. In addition to this, Hyer being lifted first, got to his second's knee in advance, while Sullivan would scarcely reach his corner and have his blanket thrown upon his shoulder, before time would be called, and he would be started to his feet. He would then run at his enemy, and irritated from his balance, would rush upon the punishment which he received. Had he been well treated, he might have preserved his temper and fought a little longer, but no treatment could have made him win. He was overmatched, and the man whom he was fighting against, exceeded all expectations, both for skill and strength. It is due to Hyer to state at this portion of our remarks, that he is not personally chargeable with any impropriety in lying on Sullivan as he did. It was his duty to lie exactly where he fell, till lifted by his seconds and carried to his corner. The question was between the seconds altogether, and the fault lay heaviest against the seconds of Sullivan himself, for not insisting more promptly and courageously on their rights. Had the other side seen that they were determined to have their man the instant he touched the ground, they would have been glad to have removed Hyer out of their way. The claim of "foul," therefore, for what was the result of their own negligence, could not stand, and Sullivan was the victim of untoward circumstances. From the first

to last, however, he had no chance to win. The reception of the first hit staggered him and his friends, while the loss of the fall after the most desperate efforts of his underhold, must have convinced him he was overmatched. There was then nothing left but desperate fighting and an instalment of revenge upon the mutual quarrel. What share he got of this, the reader has already seen, but it is our business to say, that he might have got more personal satisfaction if he had received proper care, and not been stifled out of a large portion of his time. He fought well under the circumstances, and nothing could have exceeded the courage with which he confronted an assured fate. It was a terrific struggle. The motives which governed were Ambition, Avarice, and Revenge, and the combination of such master passions could not but stimulate a bloody climax.

There never was, perhaps, a battle in which there was so much fighting in so short a space of time; none, certainly, in which more resolute punishment was given and taken, without flinching on either side. The history of the fight consists in the fact that Sullivan was overmatched; and, in the further fact that Hyer showed himself capable of matching any man of his size and weight doubtless, who exists in Britain or the United States.

SUPPLEMENTARY MATTERS.

Sullivan returned to New York on Thursday; but Hyer, in passing through Philadelphia for the same purpose, was so intoxicated with the acclamations bestowed upon him for his victory, that he suffered himself to remain over night. The result was, that he was arrested on the following morning, and on Friday, was delivered up on the requisition of the Governor of Maryland, to receive the penalties of riot with his friend Thompson, and Sullivan's trainer, O'-Donnell.

On Saturday, the following card appeared in the advertising columns of one of the N. Y. daily papers.

SULLIVAN'S NOTICE TO HIS FRIENDS.

I hereby caution my friends throughout the country who have had money staked on my fight with Hyer, not to give up a cent, as I won the fight, according to the rules of the ring, three times, and never lost it once.

JAMES SULLIVAN.

On the following day, however, this was cancelled by the following :---

YANKEE SULLIVAN'S NOTICE TO HIS FRIENDS.

The advertisement in the papers of yesterday, was not worded as I desired my friend to write it for publication. I did intend to say that, according to the rules of the ring, I had won the fight three times; but the referee thinking otherwise, I had to abide by his decision. I am sorry that my words to the gentleman, who wrote the advertisment for me, were so differently construed from my intent and meaning.

JAMES SULLIVAN.

On Monday, the Referee and Stakeholder appeared in the N. Y. *Sun*, as follows :—

CARD OF THE REFEREE.

At the contest between Thomas Hyer and James Sullivan, at Still Pond Heights, Kent County, Maryland, by the request of both parties, and the unanimous acquiescence of all present, I acted as Referee, and by said authority decided that said contest resulted in favor of Thomas Hyer, according to Articles of agreement.

S. VAN NOSTRAND.

STAKEHOLDER'S CARD.

Having been selected as stakeholder in the late contest between Hyer and Sullivan, I have deemed it necessary to publish the decision of the Referee, which decides ALL moneys staked upon the result in favor of Thomas Hyer, and I have accordingly given up the main stake of $10,000 to said Thomas Hyer.

JOHN B. FRINK.

The following extracts from the daily papers of Febuary 8th, 1849, will give an idea of the excitement manifested to learn the result of the contest, and the variety of reports in circulation :—

BY MAIL.

ARRIVAL OF TOM HYER IN PHILADEL PHIA, ETC.

PHILADELPHIA, Feb. 8, 1849.

The excitement that prevailed in the city relative to the prize fight, has subsided, in consequence of the announcement of Sullivan's defeat. This seems to gratify most of those who would have previously rejoiced that the brutal affair had been suppressed by the capture of both parties. They are satisfied that Sullivan, who has been the cause of all the prize fighting in this country for several years, should have had his comb cut and placed in the back ground among the fancy for the future.

The new champion of the ring reached the city by the train from Wilmington; and visiting the telegraph office at the Exchange, his presence there became known, and the building was besieged by an immense crowd, all anxious to gaze upon this "new lion," (if it is not a sin to call him after so noble an animal.) He will not leave the city till to-morrow.

The correct version of the fight, according to the account given by Hyer's friends, is, that it occupied only sixteen minutes, and that but fifteen rounds were fought. The situation of Sullivan is represented as being dangerous. His whereabouts is not known, but he is supposed to have been conveyed out of the bounds of Maryland, and now receiving medical treatment, probably in Delaware.

Hyer stops at Miller's Hotel, in Chesnut street, which, of course, is literally run down with the admirers of the fancy. One would not have believed that the city contained so many persons that would debase themselves, by following in the wake of such a hero.

[From the Philadelphia Bulletin, Feb. 8.]

Hyer, the victor of the brutal prize fight that came off at Rock Island yesterday afternoon, was in this city this afternoon. On going to the Exchange to send away a telegraphic dispatch, his appearance was greeted by the vociferous shouts of a large crowd, who almost carried him bodily from the cab that he was in, to the Baltimore office, up stairs, and back again to the vehicle. The cab containing him and two or three of his friends, passed the office of the Bulletin, on its way to Miller's Hotel, Chesnut street, at a quarter before 2 o'clock, P. M., followed by a crowd who seemed positively wild and frantic with excitement. The sudden coming to town of General Taylor could not have occasioned a greater *furor*. A more disgraceful scene we never witnessed in Philadelphia.

———

BY TELEGRAPH.

———

THE FIGHT.

BALTIMORE, Feb. 8,—A. M.

The fight took place yesterday about 5 P. M., at Roach's Point, Kent county, Maryland.

Sullivan is badly punished, but not dangerously.

Time occupied, about sixteen minutes.

———

BALTIMORE, Feb. 8, 1849.

The fight took place last evening at five o'clock, in Kent county, ten miles below Pool's Island.

There were but sixteen rounds. They were fought in twenty-one minutes.

Sullivan knocked Hyer down by a severe blow in the neck, which was the only knock down.

Hyer drew the first blood, from Sullivan, and in the fifteenth round wrenched his right arm.

Both of Hyer's eyes are bruised, and Sullivan's right eye is terribly hurt.

Hyer, on the sixteenth round, caught Sullivan's head under his right arm, and punished him until he was satisfied he was done for, and dropped him; when he was forcibly taken from the ring by his friends—Hyer claiming the victory, as Sullivan did not come up again in time.

It was terribly cold, and both suffered from it, as well as from the race they had from the authorities during the day.

It was one continual fight, nearly, and Hyer drew the first blood from Sullivan.

There were but a few spectators.

There is some dispute between the judges and referee ; but there seems to be no dispute as to the fact that Hyer was too much for Sullivan.

The steamer, with the military on board, is still ashore at Pool's Island.

———

BALTIMORE, Feb. 8, 1849.

Sullivan and Hyer fought, at four o'clock, yesterday afternoon, at Roach's Point, Eastern Shore, ten miles from Pool's Island.

They fought fifteen rounds in sixteen minutes.

Sullivan had the advantage the first three rounds. At the third round he knocked Hyer clean down, by a blow on the temple.

Hyer was considerably hurt by fibbing at the ropes.

At the end of the fifteenth round, Sullivan's friends withdrew him from the ring, his face having the appearance of a butcher's block.

The parties soon after left the ground. Hyer proceeded to Frenchtown, in his boat.

Hyer is not much punished.

———

BALTIMORE, Feb. 8, 1849.

The prize fight occurred yesterday in Kent county, Maryland, ten miles below Pool's Island. Sullivan was whipped in sixteen rounds, the fight lasting twenty minutes. Hyer was knocked down the first round ; both eyes were blackened. On the fifteenth round Sullivan's arm was injured, and on the sixteenth round, Hyer caught Sullivan's head under his arm, holding it there, and beating him until Sullivan's friends dragged him, whipped, from the ring.

Both the combatants, after the fight, proceeded to Wilmington : thence homeward.

The steamer Boston is still aground, with the military, police, &c., near Pool's Island.

The railroad company are about making a road over the ice in the Susquehanna.

[Telegraphic Correspondence of the Philadelphia Bulletin.]

BALTIMORE, Feb. 8, 1849.

The prize fight occurred yesterday at 4 o'clock, P. M., at Roach's Point, Kent county, Md., on the eastern shore, about ten miles below Pool's Island, the spot originally selected. Sullivan was whipped in sixteen rounds, lasting 21 minutes. Hyer was knocked down on the first round, and had both eyes blacked, and Sullivan claimed "first blood." On round third, Sullivan drove Hyer to the ropes, and, while hanging there, punished him pretty severely. Hyer, however, in round fourth, came up, half minute time, in good condition and spirits, and the rounds to the fourteenth inclusive, were fought cautiously by both, with nearly equal success. On round fifteenth, Sullivan was thrown heavily, and had his arm badly injured. Round sixteenth commenced with a desperate grapple ; Hyer caught Sullivan, drew him to him, pressed him down, caught his head "in chancery," that is, under his arm, and thus punished him, until Sullivan's friends dragged him whipped from the ring. Both parties shortly after left the ground, and proceeded toward Wilmington, via Frenchtown. Those who witnessed the fight state that Hyer, after its conclusion, was not much injured, but Sullivan was terribly battered.

The steamer Boston, with the military, police, reporters, &c., is still aground near Pool's Island. The seconds, of both Hyer and Sullivan, have been arrested in this city.

ARRIVAL OF SULLIVAN IN BALTIMORE AND HIS DEPARTURE.

BALTIMORE, Feb. 8, 1849.

Yankee Sullivan reached Baltimore this morning, and was immediately taken, by his friends, to Mount Hope Hospital ; and his life is said to be in danger.

He has a slight fracture of the skull, behind the left ear. One of his arms is broken, and his face is cut awfully. The scalp from the forehead, with the eyelid, has fallen on his cheek.

Hyer was comparatively unhurt, and walked down to the boat, whilst Sullivan had to be carried.

Tom O'Donnell and George Thompson were brought up by the police this morning, having been captured at Pool's Island, and in default of bail were committed to jail.

Hyer roped Sullivan twice, and has punished him most awfully—-every blow brought the blood.

It is supposed here that Hyer will be arrested either in Philadelphia or New York, to await the requisition of the Governor of Maryland. The precarious state of Sullivan's life, will probably lead to this.

BALTIMORE, Feb. 8—P. M.

Sullivan left the hospital this morning with his friends, after having his wounds dressed, and took the York, Pennsylvania, cars at the outer depot.

The Attorney General, Richardson, has sent despatches to all the towns on the road for his arrest and imprisonment. He is said to be seriously, but not dangerously wounded.

No tidings of his arrest yet.

ARREST OF THE SECONDS, ETC.

BALTIMORE, Feb. 8, 1849.

The steamer Boston has returned.— Thomas O'Donnell, Sullivan's trainer, and George Thompson, Hyer's second, have been arrested and are now in jail, unable to give security in the sum of $5,000 each. Sullivan is now here, in the Mount Hope Hospital, dangerously ill. One eye is out and his arm broken.

A despatch from Philadelphia, reports Hyer as saying he should have killed Sullivan if they had fought another round.

THE EXCITEMENT IN THE CITY OF NEW YORK—STREET CROWDS—GRAND ILLUMINATION IN HONOR OF TOM HYER.

The excitement which raged in the city on Wednesday, was increased on Thursday, and all down town was in a swarm, like so many bees. The news boys, always ready to reflect the spirit of the times, might be seen in pairs, setting to at every corner, and in other places where they are wont to congregate. The youngsters felt lively, for they disposed of their papers faster than they could procure them from the press; and they filled up their odds and ends of time by showing, in mimic encounters with each other, how the thing was accomplished by Hyer and Sullivan. The greatest anxiety prevailed amongst those who had made bets; and there were as many anxious faces to be seen awaiting the news, from hour to hour, as may be seen in Wall or South street, whenever a steamer arrives by which news of a fluctuating cotton or grain market is expected. There was a vast amount of money bet on the result of the fight, and all parties were anxious to know how the matter really stood.—There were hundreds and hundreds of men and boys congregated about Yankee Sullivan's house, during the whole day and up to a late hour at night. Occasional shouts were heard, and hurras for Sullivan were now and then raised; but things in that neighborhood were, for the most part, quiet. At the Fountain House, in Park Row, a grand illumination took place at night; all the windows in the front part of the house were brilliantly lighted up, and a large transparency was suspended from the second story, displaying the words—" Tom Hyer, the Champion of America." So goes the excitement, which is as yet by no means allayed.

From a New York Paper.

THE GREAT PRIZE FIGHT—ITS MORALE AND IMMORALE.

The great prize fight is finished. Tom Hyer is victorious over Sullivan; but according to the accounts which we have received, at a tremendous cost to the latter. It appears that short as was the duration of the conflict, Sullivan received so much injury as to endanger his life. The excitement which this contest has created in the public mind, is unprecedented in the annals of classical or heroic brutality, with the exception of what was caused by some particular duels with pistols that occurred in former days, the breaking out of the war with England, or subsequently that with Mexico Throughout this vast community, nothing has been heard or talked of for several days past, but the fight between Hyer and Sullivan, and the chances which each had in the contest, which took place the day before yesterday. The only exceptions to the general prevalence of this excitement were the rigidly righteous, the pious, the saints, the puritans, or those who had no time to spare from their private rogueries or pious prayers, to public matters.

This contest has presented a singular exhibition of human nature. As a question of high and lofty morality, prize fighting can only be placed on the same level with duelling, either with swords or pistols—single combats of any kind, be they with sticks or stones —or with war, either in detail, or by wholesale. Blood, wounds, damage to life and limb, and death, are the usual consequences of such exhibitions, in the ring of pugilism, the field of honor, or on the field of general battle between the armies of opposing nations. All such exhibitions and contests are contrary to the law of God, to the gospel of Christ, to the principles of humanity, as well as to the maxims of a high and sovereign morality. Still, however, it has been the weakness of human nature to indulge in such propensities, from the first fight—that between Cain and Abel, within sight of the tree of life, and within listening distance to the murmurs of the waters of Eden—through succeeding ages and centuries, to the present day. There is but little use in bemoaning the inevitable condition of humanity, or to snuffle out a condemnation against those excesses or eccentricities which seem to be part of human nature, from the first era of life to the setting of last evening's sun on the hills of the monopolising State of New Jersey. All classes of society—the rich and the poor, the high and the low, the elegantly dressed denizens of Wall street and Park Place —all shades of our heterogeneous society, were as desirous to know the result as the loafers of Chatham square or the rowdies of the Bowery. Since the famous duel between Mr. McDuffie, of South Carolina, and Col. Cummings, of Georgia—since the bloody encounter between Jonathan Silly, a member of Congress from Maine, and another from Kentucky—since the celebrated duel between Thomas S. Marshall, of Kentucky, and James Watson Webb, of New York—we have seen nothing that created so great a sensation in the public mind, which excited so much curiosity, and commanded so much attention among all classes of society, as this fight between Thomas Hyer, and Yankee Sullivan has done.

The result of the fight between Hyer and Sullivan well nigh ruined the latter, in a financial point of view, and it was a long time before he fully recovered from its effects. His friends, however, never deserted him in his misfortunes, and it was a cheering consolation to him to know that although he had lost the great battle he had not lost the confidence of his friends. Shortly after this, Mr. Sullivan, on account of some alterations being about to be made in the premises occupied by him at No. 9 Chatham street, was obliged to seek quarters elsewhere, and for this purpose secured the premises corner of Centre and Franklin streets, where he at once established himself, and his friends rallied to his support.

The mania for fighting somewhat cooled down after the great contest, and nothing of any account transpired in the prize ring until the 12th of August, 1851, when a match was fought in California, between Thompson, the trainer of Hyer, and a man named John Morrissey, not of much renown in pugilistic circles. Thompson, in order to save himself from the vengeance of an infuriated mob, should he defeat Morrissey, was obliged to submit to defeat, though

in so doing it was admitted on all sides that he acted wisely. Morrissey soon after left California, and arrived in this city, where his presence created no little excitement, and a desire to see the man who had defeated such an out-and-outer as Thompson.

It was not long before a desire was expressed by some of the "boys" to "try a hand" with the new addition to the fraternity, and several names were mentioned in connection with the affair, the most prominent of which, however, was the name of Hyer. Hyer, from a deep friendship for the man who had given so much time and attention in bringing him [Hyer] to the scratch in good order and condition, and which eventually resulted in his complete success, naturally felt indignant at the treatment Thompson had received, and so publicly expressed himself. Morrissey, elated with his late success in California, considered the remarks of Hyer of such a nature as to require some attention, and a challenge was given by Morrissey. A deposit of $100 aside was immediately made for the parties to meet and arrange matters for a match. The "Gem," in Broadway, was the spot selected for the parties to meet, and on the evening appointed, both men with their friends were present, and Hyer, being the challenged party, and not wishing to engage in battle unless it could be made an object to him, stated that he was then ready to make a match to fight Morrissey for the sum of $10,000 aside, which the latter not caring to risk, the match went off, Hyer receiving the forfeit of $100.

This little affair seemed to give new life to pugilistic matters, and it was apparent to all that a match would grow out of it. Sullivan having met Morrissey in a public house, accidentally, it was not surprising that they should notice each other, and before the parties left the house that night, a challenge passed between them, and it was arranged that on the 1st of September, 1853, the men should meet at the house corner of Whitehall and Bridge streets in this city, and make the match. On the evening in question the parties met, and the following articles were signed, and the first deposit of $250 aside made good on the spot :

Articles of Agreement for the Fight

BETWEEN

JOHN MORRISSEY AND JAMES SULLIVAN.

NEW YORK, Sept. 1. 1853.

This is to certify that I, John Morrissey, do agree to fight James Sullivan in a twenty-four foot roped ring, in strict accordance with the new rules of the London Prize Ring, in six weeks from this date, making the fight to come off on the 12th day of October, Wednesday, between the hours of 11 o'clock, A. M. and 2 o'clock, P. M., for the sum of One Thousand Dollars aside ; Two Hundred and Fifty Dollars deposited this date, September 1st; Two Hundred and Fifty Dollars to be deposited September 14th, at the house of George Kensett, between the hours of 8 and 10 P. M. ; Two Hundred and Fifty Dollars to be deposited September 28th, at the house No. 4 James street, between the hours above named ; the remaining and final deposit of Two Hundred and Fifty Dollars to be made at the house No. 324 Broadway, on the 5th day of October. And we do hereby agree that.............. shall hold the stake money in this engagement, to be given to the party receiving the decision of the referee of having won it, fairly and honorably, according to these agreements. Either party failing in the deposits, shall forfeit the amount in the stakeholder's hands. Each party on the night of the last deposit to select a man, they to choose by toss who shall name the ground of fighting, it to be within one hundred miles of the city of New York, and notice to be left with the loser of the choice, four days previous to the battle day, the 12th of October. Either party failing to be in the ring between the hours of 11 o'clock and 2 o'clock, on the 12th of October, forfeits the battle money. In case of magisterial interference, the referee shall decide the next time and place of meeting.

Signed, } JOHN MORRISSEY,
         } JAMES SULLIVAN.

The men immediately went into active training, Sullivan at the Hit-or-Miss, on the Plank Road, a few miles from Brooklyn, and Morrissey at McComb's Dam. The last deposit of $250 a side was made at the Gem on the evening of the 5th of October, and on tossing who should choose the battle ground, Morrissey was the winner. Considerable excitement was manifested throughout the city as the day approached for the gladiatorial contest. The day at last arrived, and admirers of the sport wended their way to "Boston Corners," on the line of the Harlem Railroad, about 100 miles from New York. This spot was selected by Morrissey from the supposition that it was disputed territory and that no attempts would be made to put a stop to the "business of the day." The various railroad trains from New York, Albany, and the surrounding countrys were filled with passengers, all anxious to be at "the meeting.'

At about nine o'clock on the morning of the contest great numbers of people were seen following the wagon that contained the ropes and stakes, and, having halted within a quarter of a mile of the station the "commissary" went to work, and by eleven o'clock the ring was completed, in the presence of between 2,000 and 3,000 spectators. Considerable delay now took place in consequence of the difficulty of choosing a referee, but a gentleman named Charles Allaire was selected at last, and he agreed to officiate in that capacity. At 25 minutes to 2 o'clock Morrissey made his appearance amid loud cheers, and, having shied his castor into the ring, immediately followed it, accompanied by his seconds, T. O'Donnell and "Awful" Gardner, who tied Morrissey's color to the stake; it was a long scarf, on which were emblazoned the stars and stripes of the American flag, the appearance of which was hailed with a universal cheer. Sullivan stepped into the ring, amid the hearty applause of his friends. He was waited on by William Wilson and another, the former of whom addressed the spectators, and said that all Sullivan wanted—let him win or lose---was a fair stand-up fight, and he hoped that the lookers-on would preserve order. He then proceeded to fasten Sullivan's color to the post. It was a black silk handkerchief, indicative---we presume---of "Death or Victory." Previous to setting-to, Morrissey offered to back himself for 1,000 to 800, or 500 to 400 dollars, but no one appeared willing to take him up. On proceeding to their respective corners, and "unshelling," it was evident that Morrissey had much the advantage over his opponent in age, height, and weight; in fact Sullivan appeared old enough to be his father. At seven minutes to two the men quitted their seconds' knees, and approaching each other, shook hands, and put themselves in fighting attitudes.

THE FIGHT.

Round 1.—Both men faced each other steadily, but it was soon apparent that as far as regarded science, Morrissey was a complete novice, whilst, on the contrary, Sullivan instantly threw himself into that easy London-school attitude, that bespoke the adept ; he began by feinting and stepping back, which succeeded in getting his man within his reach, when he instantly let fly with his left upon Morrissey's nose, which had the effect of tapping the claret, and drawing *first blood*. Morrissey then hit out right and left, but his blows were round and fell short. Sullivan then again made play with his left, reaching the left side of Morrisey's face, and in jumping back to avoid Morrissey's return, he slipped and went down.

Round 2.---Morrissey's face looked flushed and his nose was slightly tinged with blood when he reached the scratch He led off with his left, but was neatly stopped by Sullivan, who caught him heavily on the nose, the blood following the blow in copious streams. Some heavy exchanges then took place, which were altogether in favor of Sullivan, who eventually ended the round by going down to avoid punishment. The superior science of Sullivan was quite manifest, and his friends were in extacies.

Round 3.---Sullivan all confidence, while Morrissey's eye was much swollen and his nose bleeding profusely. They did not wait for compliments, but went at it "ding dong," Sullivan reaching Morrissey's nose at almost every offer, while the latter hit wild and without precision, although he managed to reach home on Sullivan's left eye. In return Sullivan "gave him one" where Morrissey 'chews his fodder,' by which he unfortunately split a knuckle of his left hand, which nearly disabled the further efficient use of that hand during the remainder of the contest. A clinch in Morrissey's corner, and Sullivan partly upon the ropes. He managed to slip down, however, and no damage was done.

Round 4.---This was a terrific round. Morrissey's 'mug' showed unmistakeable evidence of the handiwork of Sullivan's left ; he, nevertheless, went pluckily up to his man, and missed a well-intended blow on Sullivan's *corpus*, the latter getting nimbly away, but again advancing. Sullivan, cool and calculating, went at his man determinedly, and succeeded in planting three blows in succession upon his adversary's sore spot, without a return. At this stage of the fight Morrissey's face exhibited the most revolting appearance imaginable---his eye was dreadfully swollen and the blood was flowing in a perfect stream from each nostril. Morrissey's eye had been lanced to stop the swelling, but it was fast closing. Sullivan put in a 'one, two' on Morrissey's 'potato trap.' Morrissey now rushed at Sullivan, and planted a teazer on his sinister optic, which was soon swollen as large as an egg. Both went to work now in earnest; give and take was the order of the day, and many severe but clumsy thumps were exchanged---Sullivan at length went to grass. This was the best round of the fight.

Round 5.—Morrissey rushed on his man and inflicted a body blow; Sullivan returned the compliment with a crack on the old spot, which he repeated with another ' one, two.' Morrissey rushed at him, and caught him slightly on the shoulder as he was going down.

Round 6.—Sullivan again came up apparently weak, while Morrissey, although his face resembled a raw beefsteak, was as fresh and strong as at the start. Sullivan fought shy, as though waiting to get his wind, but every once in a while, seemingly whenever it suited him, he would send in a tremendous hit, straight from the shoulder, upon Morrissey's nose, drawing fresh blood and causing the damaged eye to swell till it was completely closed. Sullivan again tried it at the old place, but was met by a terrific smack on the chest by Morrissey's right, which nearly knocked him off his pins. Sullivan again visited Morrissey's damaged ' phiz,' and artfully went down.

Round 7.—Sullivan came up stronger ---having apparently gained his ' second wind'---and as usual commenced the round by popping in his left on Morrissey's nose. Morrissey returned, but

was short, and Sullivan repeated his favorite blow, causing the blood to flow copiously. A rally followed, in which Sullivan planted a swinging blow upon Morrissey's body. Morrissey hit out with his right, but Sullivan got away, feinted with his left, and having caught Morrissey on the ribs with his right, went down without a blow. Sullivan's left hand appeared to be damaged.

Round 8.—Sullivan getting still stronger, while Morrissey was bleeding desperately from his hurts, and even his seconds were covered with blood. A little sparring, when a rally took place, in which Sullivan delivered some terrible body blows and finally went down, himself untouched.

Round 9.—Sullivan opened the game by planting a sharp hit on the old wounds of Morrissey, jumped back, put in another, stopped Morrissey's return and got in a third. Then some counter-hitting took place, in which Sullivan had the best of it, as Morrissey seemed to hit short. Sullivan down, as usual.

Round 10.—Sullivan's left eye was now almost gone, which, Morrissey perceiving, he placed a severe blow on the damaged ogle with his right, but napped it in return again on the nose from Sullivan's left, who knocked Morrissey's ' pimple' about as he pleased, but with little apparent effect. Sullivan finally got his left in on Morrissey's ribs and went down.

Round 11.—Sullivan very wary, his left hand being injured and his left peeper quite shut up. Sullivan's seconds cautioned him to keep out, and take it easy; that he must surely win if he would only be careful. Sullivan went to work at the face: but he received a tremendous body blow from Morrissey, which made his side crack like a whip. He, however, did not seem to mind it, and rapped away at Morrissey's face as vigorously as ever, closing the round by falling.

Round 12.—Sullivan planted a heavy right-hander on his opponent's under 'desoculator,' which was removed a considerable distance from its proper place, and increased its magnitude to an alarming extent. Morrissey rushed wildly on Sullivan, getting in on Sullivan's eye. Sullivan then went down.

Round 13.—Short round. Sullivan got his 'one, two' again in on Morrissey's ' snuff box.' Morrissey rushed at him and seized him, but Sullivan slipped through his hands like an eel. and went down.

Round 14.—Another short round. Sullivan planted two stinging hits òn the nose of his adversary and received a return on his much disfigured cheek. He went down as before.

Round 15.—This was a truly desperate round. Morrissey, being told by his second to 'go in,' rushed at his man, but Sullivan, too leary, slipped on one side, nailing Morrissey with a terrific salute on the ribs. Morrissey, nothing daunted, followed him up and got Sullivan with his back across the ropes in such a position, that, had he known more of ' ring fighting,' in all probability he might have finished the fight at once; but, from some unknown cause, he relinquished his advantage, and Sullivan slipped down.

Round 16.—Short round. Sullivan feinted with his left, caught Morrissey on the ribs with his right, and went down

Round 17.---Morrissey was urged by his seconds to go in and fight, while Sullivan's seconds advised him to keep out. Severe punishment administered on both sides. Sullivan ultimately dropped down [cheers for both parties.]

Round 18.---Sullivan at his accustomed ' dodge,' feinted with the left, and catching Morrissey with his right, went down with the blow, Morrissey derisively pointing at him.

Round 19.---Morrissey, seeing his opponent weak, dashed in two body blows, when Sullivan got down.

Round 20 ---Sullivan succeeded in drawing Morrissey, who rushed in, but was met by Sullivan, when both went to hard work, and each had his share of punishment. Sullivan again down.

Round 21.---The friends of Morrissey still offered to bet even that he would win, notwithstanding all he had received, relying entirely on his great powers of endurance. Morrissey led off, but

was stopped. He tried again, and caught Sullivan on the damaged eye, which entirely shut out daylight. Sullivan got in two or three more on Morrissey's awful looking countenance and fell.

Round 22.---This was a good fighting round, hard hitting on both sides. Sullivan, as usual, went down .

Round 23.---Morrissey made play. Sullivan on the retreat, yet he contrived to plant a double ' one, two' on his opponent's unfortunate conk. Morrissey in a rush caught Sullivan a stinger on his damaged check, which nearly grassed him, but recovering his equilibrium he ' returned to the charge.' Morrissey aimed a swinging right-hander at him, which Sullivan perceiving,slipped down, and avoided it.

Round 24.—A hard round. They both went at it in earnest as soon as they reached the score, and countered away on the heads of each other. Sullivan repeated his favorite visitations several times on Morrissey's beak, and received one or two in return. Sullivan down again.

Round 25.—Sullivan continued to hit his man on the ' raw' with his left, and on the body with the right, but always dropped at the approach of danger.

Round 26.—Sullivan again at the old spot, and before Morrissey could reach with his return, Sullivan was down.

Round 27.—Sullivan on approaching the scratch, asked his opponent if he was Champion now. Neither man did much damage in this round. Sullivan got in a body blow, and fell.

Round 28.—Sullivan, rather wildly, hitting at the ' old spot,' and getting down in the ' old style.'

Round 29.—Pretty much in the same style as the previous round.

Round 30.—Morrissey got in a couple of smacks on Sullivan's frontispiece, but in return received principal and interest ; 2 to 1 on Sullivan.

Round 31.—Pretty much in Sullivan's favor. Sullivan getting down, to avoid punishment.

Round 32.—Sullivan commenced at the face and Morrissey countered him ; several hard counter hits were exchanged. Then Sullivan broke away, and put in three or four smacks on Morrissey's face as he followed him, and fell. It was a sickening sight to see Morrissey at the end of this round—the blood gushing in streams from nose, mouth, and half a dozen gashes on his face. The left side of Sullivan's head was very large.

Round 33.—Morrissey slow, and seemed week in the knees. Sullivan opened on the face and could put in blows where he chose. After giving Morrissey four or five hits and receiving one on the cheek, he fell, after a swinging right hand hit on Morrissey's ribs.

Round 34.—Sullivan got in at least a dozen sharp hits in this round on Morrissey's face, and fell in hitting at the body.

Round 35.—Sullivan put in two right hand hits, and, receiving a slight rap on the sore cheek, fell.

Round 36—Sullivan went up to Morrissey, who appeared wild and weak in the legs, and struck him when and where he chose. His blows were not so forcible as at first, but yet too much for human nature to endure much longer; and although Morrissey was bearing up manfully, proving himself as game a man as ever stood up in a ring, it was evident that he was failing rapidly. His knees shook, and his hands were low, and his mind bewildered.

Round 37, and last.—The appearance of Morrissey, who looked much more injured than he really was, gave increased confidence to Sullivan, who at once rushed at Morrissey, getting in a slight tap on the sore spot. Morrissey dashed after him, and before Sullivan could drop, caught him with his arm round the neck, and rushed him to the ropes, where he had him in an awkward position. Sullivan endeavored to extricate himself, and succeeded in turning Morrissey by a very clever manœuvre. Morrissey's seconds, judging foul play had been practised by the seconds of Sullivan, rushed in to the assistance of their man. In a moment the seconds were engaged in a warfare among themselves; the ring was broken in, and a general battle seemed inevitable. "Time" was called, and Morrissey, hearing the call, very quickly appeared at the scratch; but Sullivan was knocking out right and left among the seconds and friends of his opponent, and did not hear the call, and the time allowed for the appearance of the men at the scratch after the "call" having elapsed, and probably 2 or 3 minutes besides, without Sullivan confronting Morrissey, the latter appealed to the Referee, who decided in favor of Morrissey. Morrissey then left the ring, and Sullivan, having got through with his other little matters heard "time" called again, and went up to the scratch, but it was too late—the Referee had given his decision, and from that decison there could be no appeal. There was great dissatisfaction expressed when the decision was made known, and it was looked upon as an extraordinary proceeding.

The fight lasted 55 minutes, and during that time Morrissey received punishment enough to have satisfied almost any man, but at the call of time he was always on hand, and never flinched from the blows dealt him by Sullivan. Sullivan had greatly the advantage, owing to his experience in prize fighting, and his knowledge of every move in the science of pugilism.

The sudden decision of the referee took all by surprise, as Sullivan, at the time, had all the best of the fight; and if continued for a few rounds more, Morrissey would have been blind. Whilst Morrissey could see, and come up to time, he was no doubt a dangerous customer, being a game and a resolute fellow, possessed of sound bottom, and a formidable hitter with his right hand, but as to pugilistic skill he is totally ignorant of it, as also of the rules of the P. R., and lost many opportunities of winning the battle, through a timid apprehension of hitting a foul blow. Sullivan, on the contrary, proved himself to be perfectly *au fait* to all the tactics of the Ring. Had all the seconds kept their places in the corners till the round was finished, the fight no doubt, would have come to a better conclusion. The referee did not appear to know his duty, and had no right to give his decision until order was restored, and he had been appealed to by the umpires.

Sullivan published a card, cautioning his friends not to give up the money bet on him, &c., and the following challenge also appeared about the same time :

CHALLENGE TO JOHN MORRISSEY.

It is entirely unnecessary for me to state that I fairly and undisputably was the winner of our last contest, twenty-five hundred disinterested persons being present, and all, but perhaps ten interested ones, being satisfied that such was the fact. But, in order to convince the public and your few prejudiced friends that I am your superior in a twenty-four foot ring contest and in liberality, I am willing to give the disputed money to any charitable institution, viz : Fire Department Widows' and Orphans' Fund, or to any other charitable object you can name, and make a new match to meet you again for $5,000, to come off within six weeks from this day.   Man and money ready at my house, 82½ Chatham street.

JAMES SULLIVAN,
Champion, not Irvin's champion.

The following is Morrissey's reply :

" A CARD.—I would not unnecessarily intrude myself or my opinions upon the notice of the public on matters relative to prize fighting. But a sense of justice to myself, compels me, under present circumstances, to reply to the challenge of James Sullivan, which appeared in the Herald of yesterday. In addition to his challenge, he makes a most singular proposition, to give away the money which I have fairly won under the rules of the prize ring, and according to the decision of the referee ; and what is more to the purpose, I have the money now in my pocket. Mr. Sullivan may be a very charitable man ; but a proposition on his part to give away my money to some charitable institution, is, indeed, a stretch of liberality unprecedented among prize-fighters, and one that I am not willing to acknowledge or subscribe to, when it is made entirely at my expense. Such tricks are too stale in this community, and the proposition will, no doubt, be properly appre-

ciated. In answer to the challenge of Mr. Sullivan, I will state that I am ready and willing to make the match for $5,000 aside, at a proper time and place, in four months from this time, and all I ask is fair play, for I am willing to go far enough from New York, or any other city where crowds cannot come to interfere with the fight.   I will also add, as a bonus on my part, $500 to the stake-money, which he, Sullivan, can give to some charitable institution, after he wins it. He can now have an opportunity to gratify his ardent desire to whip me in a ring, and will also be enabled to exercise the charitable inclinations of his benevolent heart, to the extent of five-hundred dollars at my expense. If Sullivan wants to fight me, he knows where I can be found. If he intends to play the braggadocio before the public, he may have that part all to himself.

JOHN MORRISSEY.

The above cards amounted to nothing, however, for about that time our moral papers made a desperate onslaught upon the authorities for not arresting the principals in the fight at 'Boston Corners.' Sullivan, at the same time, concluded to give up prize fighting, and retire from the Pugilistic Ring. The following is his communication on the subject.

SULLIVAN'S RETIREMENT FROM THE RING.

New York, Oct. 24, '53.

TO THE EDITOR OF THE N. Y. CLIPPER :

SIR :—I was surprised at seeing a card from the would-be Champion, censuring the editors and reporters of newspapers for doing their duty in an honest and upright manner. Every one knows that this great, big, wooden man was no more in my hands than a shuttle-cock. He certainly did get the decision of the Referee, but how did he manage to get it ? Jim Irwin, who never won a shilling honest in his life, can best tell. The man has the impudence to call me a braggadocio. I leave that to every man in New York, friend or foe, to judge. I have fought six battles in New York, five of which I won, and the smallest of those with whom I fought was 25lbs. heavier than myself. One of them I consider no man on earth could have fought much longer than I did, nor harder. Now I would advise this would-be fighting man to go to some other business besides fighting, as he will never become a star of that water, for if he could not lick a man forty-one years old, thirty pounds lighter, and three inches shorter than himself, he ought to hang up his fiddle.

For my part, *I am done forever entering the Prize Ring as a Principal*, such being the wish of all my friends, who are all satisfied that I have done enough. But to give him a chance to show his pluck, which I doubt he has got but very little, I will match a man against him, who, at this time does not weigh 150 pounds, and he to be 160 pounds, for $1000, if he can get any one fool enough to back him ; I will also give him his own time, but I must not have Allaire for Referee.

N. B.—I hope no one who bet on me will be fool enough to give up one cent of the money on the decision of the Referee, as it was all a sham to get the outside bets. I have sued the stakeholder for the recovery of the money, that I know honestly belongs to me.

JAMES SULLIVAN,

CHAMPION,

No, 82½ Chatham street.

The stakes, after much discussion, were finally given up to Morrissey, and thus ended the 'Fight at Boston Corners.'

In consequence of the outcry made by the 'moralists' of New York, warrants were issued for the arrest of the principals and seconds in the battle, and Morrissey and his seconds suddenly left for parts unknown. Sullivan, however, was not so fortunate. He was arrested on the 3d of November, on a requisition from the Governor of Massachusetts, and conveyed out of this city, on Saturday, 5th November, and finally lodged in the jail at Lenox, Berkshire County, Mass., where he remained one week, at the expiration of which time he was released after giving bail in the sum of $1500 to appear, when wanted. Sullivan's old opponent, Hyer, was his greatest friend in this last difficulty, and escorted him back to New York on the completion of his visit to the Yankees.

Mr. Sullivan is now quietly engaged in attending to the wants of his customers at his house, No. 82½ Chatham street, and those who favor him with a call will meet with courteous treatment from all engaged about the establishment. We wish him every success.

TOM HYER'S
FIRST FIGHT.

FULL REPORT OF THE GALLANT CONTEST BETWEEN

TOM HYER AND COUNTRY M'CLEESTER,

9th September, 1841.

The antagonist of Hyer, in his first fight, was the celebrated John McCleester, more generally known as *Country McClusky*, recently deceased. The fight between these two men originated in a private feud, which was brought to a determination by a visit of McCleester to Hyer, in Park Row, on the night of the 8th of September, 1841, and a proposal that they should go over into the Park and fight their differences out. Hyer, however, unwilling to incur the consequences of such a breach of the peace, refused, and proposed a spot on the North River, which, after some chaffering, was acceded to ; and it was agreed, that each should meet the next morning on the Albany boat, accompanied by a small number of friends. They then retired to their beds to refresh themselves as best they could, for the terrible business of the morrow. In the morning they were both on board the boat at the appointed hour, and in due time were left at Cauldwell's Land-ing, a small place up the North River. They did not search long for a stopping place, for a climb of about one hundred yards up a steep hill near the shore brought them to a natural platform, which was exactly the spot for the business in hand. They commenced at once to strip, and the seconds proceeded to adjust some matters which had not yet been arranged. As the fight was for a settlement of a quarrel, and as a suspicion had been raised by their respective enemies as to the game of either man, to thoroughly test it, it was agreed by all parties, that it should be a fair ring fight, at half minute time, all blows to be considered fair, so that neither, upon becoming tired of the work, or afraid to continue, should resort to a foul blow to end the contest. This left no alternative but desperate fighting. J. Somerindyke and A. Reynolds were the seconds of Hyer; and Alick Hamilton his bottle holder. McClusky was attended by Sullivan and Ketchum as seconds, and Nesbitt as bottle holder. No ring was made, but the men ran into a scratch drawn by Somerindyke, to which they were called at five minutes past eleven.

THE MEN.

Upon coming up both looked well, though Country's flesh appeared more clear and compact than Hyer's, which was ruddy, and though not loose, not firm. Hyer has the advantage of a greater length of reach than his antagonist and is three inches taller, straight, symmetrical, lithe and sinewy, and altogether a perfect model of a man for his weight: which is 176 lbs. Country is more soggy, but possessed of fine gladiatorial points, as some future combats may find to his cost. His weight is 160 lbs. He is a hard working man, and previous to this encounter is said to have returned from a long voyage before the mast; so his condition might be considered tolerably good. Hyer, on the contrary, had been irregular in his mode of living, and has indulged during the last two years in a life of leisure, but little conducive to the vigor which it was necessary for him, on this occasion, to possess.

THE FIGHT.

Round 1. On coming up the odds were 20 to 30 on Hyer. Upon taking his position, he stood firm and erect, and his hands well up and his head moderately forward. Country also stood well up, though his manner was not as easy as Hyer's. A slight, but wicked smile was perceptible on the lips of each, which spoke more mischief than a thousand frowns, and they came to the scratch readily and free. Hyer waited for the assault, keeping his arms playfully free, and ready for a fly. Country advanced, made a left hand pass, was stopped, and Hyer caught him on the left cheek (first blow from Hyer,) Country then rallied sharply, a clinch followed, and he was thrown.

Round 2. Both came up eagerly, and Country led off left and right, in double quick time, and succeeded in planting a heavy blow over Hyer's eye, which split it and started the claret (first blood for Country) Hyer returned with interest in a desperate rally, and at the conclusion went to the ground by a body blow. Country hurt his right hand severely in this round.

Round 3. Hyer stopped with his left hand, made a charge, clinched, and threw M'C. heavily.

Round 4. Hyer at it right away with his left upon Country's fifth rib ; C. answered on the breast, but caught a hard blow on the jaw again in return. A clinch and tussle ensued, during which they top-knotted severely. They closed and tussled again, and Country went down with Hyer upon him.

Round 5. Hyer hit slightly with his left and right, and caught it severely on the collar bone in return ; which, however, he answered by a tremendous body blow ; a clinch followed, and Country went heavily to the ground.

Round 6. Country led off right and left, and brought Hyer to the ground in a clean and handsome manner by a body blow.

Round 7. Smart counter hits right and left ; Hyer caught a heavy body blow, they clinched, and Country went down hard.

Round 8. Several exchanges, a rally, terrific fighting all over the ring ; Hyer clinched, and after a short tussle threw Country very heavy.

Round 9. Country made a rush, got in a heavy body blow on the left side (his favorite point) which H. returned with tremendous force on the mouth, and received a severe jaw breaker in return, immediately followed up by another of the same sort, though somewhat lighter ; then followed a brisk exchange right and left, the last of which from Country brought Hyer down clean. This round lasted 9 minutes.

Round 10. Smart exchanges ; a break ---Hyer gathered cautiously for a fly, let loose, and caught Country a terrible right hander on the eye. Country then made a rush and caught Hyer like a Paixhan bomb on the lip and carried him to the ground, hurting his right hand again with the blow.

Round 11. Up to this time Country might be said to have had the advantage, but he now gave evident signs of distress; but Hyer, freshening with his punishment, went to work in earnest; he struck fiercely and with tremendous execution; the last blow fell upon C'.s eye badly; Hyer then ran in, clinched, threw and fell heavily upon him.

Round 12. Wild exchanges—a rally and C. went to the ground. Five rounds of hard fighting and alternate success here followed, the last one ending in a clinch, which resulted in C. falling back.

Round 18. The intervening rounds up to this one were not marked by anything of a specially interesting character. On coming up this time Country opened the ball, but was stopped left and right. H. returned and C. caught it badly in two visitations on the mouth, returned by a body blow from C. in his favorite spot on the left; followed by a clinch and C.'s overthrow.

Round 19. Sharp rally, counter hits ending in a mutual blow which brought both to the ground at once.

Round 20. Hyer led off but Country got away; slight counter; Country retreated, but waiting for his opportunity rallied and got in a heavy body blow; Hyer followed threatening mischief. Country rallied again, reeled, slipped and fell.

Round 21. Heavy exchanges, a clinch, a break, hard hitting, another clinch and Country down.

Round 22. Desperate fighting and both down.

The next five rounds were short, and consisted of sharp exchanges of body blows, each round resulting in a throw, three to Country and two to Hyer; indeed a clinch usually resulted in favor of the latter.

Round 28. Country now began to breathe with difficulty and to show evident signs of fatigue, while Hyer, on the contrary, appeared to freshen with his work; he tried left, but C. got away. C. advanced, hit round, but struck short, and went to the ground with a collar bone blow.

Round 29. Both came up well, C. led off and after a brisk rally brought H. to the ground.

Round 30. Country's friends, a little cheered by this, encouraged their man by saying—" You've got him now, Country; give him one of them old Chatham Square fellows." "Yes, he has!" returned Hyer, ironically, accompanying the remark by a wink to his party at the same time that he was gathering for a spring. The thunder did not rumble for nothing, for down it came in a tremendous visitation on the left side of Country's nose, which sent the blood spirting out of it in streams, and appeared to have literally split it in two. The blow struck C. clean down.

Round 31. Country showed his punishment by his distress. The fight was now plainly Hyer's, and 20 to 5 was offered on him and taken two or three times. H. led off, a rally followed, ending in a clinch and C. went down again.

Round 32. Terrible right hand blow on H.'s ribs, which were now dreadfully swollen from repeated hitting; a clinch, hit again, and H. went down.

Round 33. A rally, clinch, and McC. thrown.

Round 34. Close fighting, hard hitting, and McC. down by a neck blow.

Round 35. A rally, close hitting and McC. thrown. H. standing firm.

Eight rounds followed in favor of H., in which he went down to the ground three times.

Round 44. Heavy exchanges. H. gathered for a charge, let fly with tremendous force and caught C. on the top of the head. Such was the power of this blow that it split Country's head completely open and sent the blood gushing out in streams. It was the opinion of several on the ground, that had his head not luckily have been down, this visitation would have killed him. It was followed by another of the same sort and C. was struck down.

Round 45. Counter hits, a rally and both down.

Round 46. H. led off on C.'s ribs, C. returned with a round blow in the old spot.

Round 47. Both hit, a rally, a clinch and McC. thrown.

Round 48. Short round, some hitting, a close and both down.

‧ Round 49. A desperate rally, a heavy blow on H.'s ribs, a rally and both down.

Round 50. Hard hitting, a rally and H. down.

Round 51. A rally, clinch and McC. down.

Round 52. Sharp fighting, H. down.

Round 53. Wild fighting, a clinch, both down.

Round 54. Hard fighting, a clinch, a break, counter hits struck, H. down.

Round 55. A short rally, McC. down.

The next six consisted of hard fighting and a good exchange of body blows, those by Country in his old spot. In the 62d round, Country caught a smacking cut on the cheek which brought him to the ground. Varying success followed until the 69th.

Round 69. Country led off with his right, but caught it in return on the ear; a close followed, they broke, Hyer made a pass with his right, was thrown off, and received a blow on the old place on the side, which told so powerfully as to start the blood through the flesh.

Round 70. A rally and Hyer dropped.

Round 71. Light exchanges and Hyer down.

Round 72. H. struck down and C. floored by the recoil.

Round 73. Both fatigued. Country suffering very much. Hyer advanced, made an offer with his right hand, was thrown off, when a mutual blow was hit that brought both to the ground, and while they lay thus, Hyer, with a smile and good natured remark of "put it there, old fellow," reached out his arm and heartily shook hands with his antagonist.

Round 74. A rally, Hyer to work right and left, C. down.

Round 75. C. down on his knees, up again and knocked down.

Round 76. H. hit over C.'s shoulder with his left, was caught and struck down.

Then followed six rounds, in which there was some short, hard hitting by both, though everything was manifestly in favor of Hyer, whose blows went heavily in, while Country, from his exhausted state, made rather shoves than blows.

Round 83. Country tried with his left and right, but got nothing in. Hyer advanced, struck out, and carried him down with a head blow.

Round 84. Wild exchanges with no effect. C. down.

Round 85. A rally; short, hard hits. H. down.

Round 86. Hyer led off, hitting C. on the mouth and nose with his right, and repeating it on the ear with his left. C. down.

Round 87. A guinea to a shilling on Hyer. Country was nearly gone, and nothing but his thorough game continued the fight; still he made a good show, and managed to carry Hyer down at the end of a brisk rally.

Round 89. Poor Country came up gasping, but free; he could, however, make no show at all; the day was against him, and he was striking against fate. He went down.

Round 90. Country came up groggy, but exhibited unflinching game. Hyer succeeded in planting some heavy blows in his mug, and he went down again.

Round 91. Slight counter hits, a rally, and H. went down with a light body blow.

Round 92. A short recovery. Sharp hits right and left, and Country down flying.

Round 93. Country lay gasping in the arms of his seconds, who plainly saw that all hopes of a favorable change were extinguished. He was evidently in a helpless state, and able only to receive punishment. To save him from further unnecessary suffering, his seconds determined to draw him; but the indomitable and true hearted fellow begged in the most earnest manner to be allowed to go in once more.

Round 94. C. staggered up, made a pass with his left, was caught, and went down flying. Here his seconds would have drawn him again, but he begged as before, and was allowed the *privilege.*

Round 95. Wild hitting. C., dreadfully jobbed, went down by a head blow

Round 96. C. came up quite groggy, while Hyer appeared to freshen. He struck out with tremendous effect, caught C. on the jaw, and carried him down. Further effort was of no use to Country; he offered scarcely any resistance to Hyer, whatever, who hit him when and where he pleased. From this round to the 101st, Country's seconds endeavored to draw him, but suffered themselves to give way to his desires to try it once more. In the 100th round, Hyer, who for the time had lost his usual self command, seconded his entreaties with a " O let him come in, let him come in; I'll kill him this time." A neck blow followed this remark, that made Country's collar bone ring again. In the 101st, Country met with the same treatment, when Sullivan would listen to him no longer, but drew him at once, stating that he had lost the fight, and resigning his claim to the stake. Hyer was now left the victor of a hard fought field of 101 rounds, which occupied three hours, five minutes less. Country retired, dreadfully punished, weak, and tottering; Hyer looked fresh, and capable of fighting an hour or two more.

"The manner in which the match was fought," says the Sporting Chronicle of that date, "reflects the highest honor on the two combatants; the rounds were not made by dodging and dropping without a hit, but were clear knock down ones, all. It was, by far, a harder battle than the celebrated one between Brassey and Parker, on the 10th August last, which was so much talked of in the English papers, for it was a continuous and desperate planting of foul blows and fair, without interruption, and the fight lasted five minutes longer. Some experienced pugilists were on the ground, and declare the fight one of the best that ever came off in the country: and under the circumstances, Hyer's condition being considered, perhaps the best. Hyer is but 22 years of age. He is, however, no fighting man, and does not wish to be so considered; on the contrary, he refuses ever to fight another match. Not many, we imagine, will interfere with his having his way."

FATAL PRIZE FIGHT

BETWEEN

LILLY AND M'COY,

AT HASTINGS, N. Y., ON TUESDAY, SEPT. 13, 1842.

The fight between Christopher Lilly and Thomas McCoy originated at a sparring exhibition in the Bowery, where both parties met shortly after the former's victory over Murphy. They had been old acquaintances, and there was an unsettled grudge between them. Amid the general encomiums bestowed on the youthful conqueror, McCoy's voice was silent, and when challenged for his opinion, he gave it in opposition to the prevailing sentiment. This Lilly couldn't bear, and feeling desirous to brush away any existing doubt from his rival's mind, asked Tom to put the gloves on with him for a set-to and try. But the latter refused, and in an instant, Lilly hit him a straightforward blow that carried him to the floor. McCoy rose and rushed in, but they were soon separated, and a match was instantly proposed. Everything was soon arranged ; a deposit was, either that evening or the next day, made, and each party went in active training—McCoy into the hands of James Sandford, and Lilly in the care of McGee.

On Tuesday morning, 13th Sept., 1842, the appointed time, the fight came off according to the articles of agreement.

The morning was just such a one as people generally prefer for not intruding upon, as the rain poured in torrents, the consequence of which was, that not one-fourth of the number that witnessed the fight between Sullivan and Bell were in attendance. The steamboat Saratoga, (McCoy's;) Indiana, (Lilly's ;) Boston, Gazelle, Napoleon and Conroy, were all chartered to convey passengers to the spot selected for the fight, and between eight and nine oclock, as the rain ceased and the sun began to show himself, these boats took their departure from the city with only 1500 passengers. They proceeded up the Hudson about twenty miles, to a spot selected about half way betweeen Yonkers and Hastings, in Westchester Co. The position of the ground was excellent, being on a flat, lying between the Croton Acqueduct and the Hudson, slightly declining, and thus giving an amphitheatrical view from the ropes to the top of the reservoir. The termination of the sublime scenery of the pallisades opposite, the view of the noble Hudson, the villages of Piermount and Nyack, in the distance, on the opposite shore, and the exciting scene in the immediate vicinity, all tended to render the place selected as the very best spot that could have been chosen for the occasion, adding as it did to the comfort and convenience of all present. The arrangements in and about "the spot" were also good, there being two large outside rings shielding the "twenty-four feet square" from the crowd; the time was now drawing near when the men were to enter the ring, and every man was looking for a place to view the fight.

The following account of the men and the battle is given by an eye-witness.

THE MEN.

Lilly is said to weigh 140, though many believe him to reach as high as 145 lbs. ; he is twenty three years of age, and an inch taller than his antagonist. On stripping, he presented a fine appearance. His skin was very clear and light in color, but firm in texture and healthy in tone. His form is round almost to perfection; his sides, instead of branching from the waist, gradually outwards to the arm-pits, circle concavely inwards like reversed crescents; his neck is strong and muscular in a high degree; his head—a fighting one, remarkably well set—small, round, bony, with a small featured dial, and his underworks, though at first somewhat light to the eye, are sufficiently strong for endurance.

If Lilly's appearance was fine, McCoy's was beautiful. His skin had a warmer glow than the former's ; his form was more elegantly proportioned, and his air and *style* more graceful and manlike. His swelling breast curved out like a cuirass; his shoulders were deep, with a bold curved blade, and the muscular development of the arm large and finely brought out. His head was rather large and long, yet it indicated courage and a love for strife, and the manner in which it was set betokened strength. He was but twenty years and two months old, and weighed 137lbs.

THE FIGHT.

Lilly first entered the ring, attended by Ford and McCleester, the former seconds of Yankee Sullivan in both his battles ; and on tossing up his cap, was warmly greeted with cheers from his side of the ring. McCoy soon after followed, with James Sanford and Henry Shanfroid, and on following suit with his castor, was greeted in like manner. While they were stripping, the interest was so great, that every man on the ground appeared to have a desire to stake something on the issue, and even bets, to a large amount, were made. Neither man could be said to be the favorite, for of the ten or twelve thousand dollars that were certainly known to be "up," all was evenly wagered. After the men were peeled, the Judges and Referee were selected, the toss was made for the choice of position and won by McCoy, who took the rising ground, though with it he had the sun directly in his eyes. When all was ready, McCoy went over to Lilly, and pulling out two bank notes of $100 each, wagered it with the latter; then both shook hands across with the seconds, retired to their corners, and awaited the cry of "havoc."

Round 1. 1 o'clock, exactly. At the call of "time," both came directly up, neither offering the customary hypocrisy of a greeting. They sparred with some caution for a time; at length, McCoy slightly advanced across the scratch and watching his chance, let fly with his left, but was stopped. Lilly then shifted his ground, when McCoy closed, and during a short struggle, in which each endeavoured to fib, the latter was heavily thrown. Lilly rose unhurt and McCoy went smiling to his corner, with blood trickling from his left ear. (Shrieks of "first blood!" "hey, go it my Lilly !" from Sullivan and others in Lilly's corner.) Between this round and the next, a person said to be a magistrate of the county was pointed out to me, who appeared to be remonstrating with Sullivan and others; but on "time" being called I was obliged to withdraw my attention, and saw no more.

2. McCoy came up eagerly and with a remark of " You aint got old Murphy to deal with now," struck out, caught Lilly on the breast, but received a tremendous visitation on the mouth; in return, in straining forward to answer it, McCoy slipped and went down.

3. Some wary sparring and shifting about ; at last Lilly hit out and caught McCoy severely on the neck, from which McCoy slipped down on his knee, Lilly smiling at him.

4. Both wary, McCoy giving ground and showing slight fatigue, Lilly made a slight push out at McCoy's breast, and

McCoy went down. (Laughter and cries of "Bah! bah!" from Sullivan and Lilly's friends.)

5. Lilly came briskly in and went right to work, caught McCoy again on the mouth; McCoy countered and fell. (cries of "*foul*.")

5. Both eager, heavy exchanges by both, right and left: McCoy then rushed in, when Lilly chopped him with his right severely on the back; Tom, however, soon stopped this work, and in a short violent struggle both went to the ground, side by side.

7. McCoy came up,

"———his lip and neck's pure dyes ———dabbled with the deep blood which ran o'er,"

showing an eager desire to fight. In return to a pass he made, Lilly struck out with his left, caught his man in the abdomen, from which the latter fell, and rose from the ground pointing at his stomach and complaining of a "foul" blow. An uproar immediately ensued; the two parties violently charging and denying, during which the Judges agreed that the blow *was* "foul," and on appealing to the Referee, had their decision affirmed by him. Here the fight should have ended But the principal backer of McCoy, from excess of generosity, refused what he called "an advantage," and though the decision was worth some thousands to him, demanded that the contest should go on. In the interim, some one had called "time," and the men, by appearing at the scratch, concluded all foregone exceptions.

8. Lilly led off with a sharp cheek blow, followed by a tremendous repeater on McCoy's mouth; McCoy then rushed in, and after a few sharp exchanges, closed, endeavored to throw Lilly, who turned him, however, as he was going down, and fell heavily on him.

9. Lilly came up bleeding freely at the nose—they went at it fiercely, and planted a heavy mutual hit; a little sparring and another counter followed, ending in a clinch, each firmly locking the other's hands. A dispute ensued, both claiming "foul"—considerable time elapsed, at the end of which, in obedience to the numerous cries of "fight! fight!" they struggled violently together,

and McCoy was again turned under, with Lilly on him.

10. McCoy put in a severe body blow, and in following with the other hand over-reached himself and fell.

11. Even bets freely offered on McCoy—Lilly looking flimsy and distressed. McCoy came up smiling and confident, received a hit from Lilly on the chin, rallied and closed on him. Lilly caught him well and both fibbed severely, a struggle ensued, at the end of which Lilly turned McCoy and fell on him as before.

12. McCoy smiling and speaking in an under tone to his antagonist, as he squared up to him. "$100 to $80 on McCoy!" Cautious sparring: both struck out, and both stopped the ugly looking threatened visitations. McCoy made another heavy offer, which not getting home, in consequenc of a quick aside movement of Lilly's, threw him forward, badly off his guard, which Lilly took advantage of by giving him a sharp upper cut as he fell. This was done in a careless and rather contemptuous manner, as if he would say, "There, take that for your stupidity!" (Cheers for Lilly.)

13. Tremendous counter—rush by both, and heavy exchanges, clinch, and McCoy down at the ropes.

14. "$100 to $60 on McCoy!" This offer, though McCoy had no perceptible advantage of Lilly, was not taken; Lilly's friends fearing, probably, that there was something more in it than met the eye. McCoy came up full of confidence, exclaiming, "Ah, I've got you now, old fellow, sure!" and planted two sounding body blows "Yes, you have!" answered Lilly scornfully, and following up the remark, made a hit at Mac's mouth which made everything ring again. McCoy, at this, rushed madly in and closed; but after receiving some severe punishment from Lilly's right on the small of the back, he was turned and the latter fell heavily on him.

15. Heavy countering. Lilly hit out below the belt, as low as the groin, but was stopped by McCoy. (Cries of "foul.") Lilly hit again, closed and threw McCoy, and fell heavily upon him. McCoy on getting up, complained of being "hit

foul;" the Judges saw it, and were again agreed, and loud cries of "foul" were shouted from all parts of the ring. Lilly's seconds defended him by saying that the blow was "thrown off," and McCoy's backers again passed away their right, by declaring they wanted no such advantage.

16. Heavy body blow thrown in by McCoy,—returned on the mouth by Lilly twice successively. McCoy rallied, rushed in, and sharp fibbing ensued by both—they then broke, exchanged another hit, closed again, and after a brief struggle, McCoy threw Lilly heavily, and fell on him. (Cheers and "$100 to $60 on McCoy!")

17. Lilly hit out weak, in answer to a light body blow from McCoy; he made another pass, and McCoy dropped.— (Hisses, and cries of "bah! bah!")

18. McCoy got in a light body blow, and dropped away from a wicked return.

19. Lilly improving—McCoy got in his usual body blow, which was returned by Lilly heavily in the old place on the mouth. Heavy counters—Lilly getting in a terrific lunge on McCoy's left eye; a close by McCoy followed, who, in trying to throw Lilly, was turned himself, and fell heavily, with his antagonist upon him. The fight had now lasted 20 minutes.

20. Cautious sparring. In getting away from threatened danger, Lilly slipped on his knee—rose, followed, and delivered a stinging hit on Mac's lip, cutting it badly, and starting the blood out in streams. McCoy returned with a heavy lunge full on Lilly's frontal bone. Lilly then attempted to rush in, but short, quick exchanges followed, ending in a clinch, and McCoy was heavily thrown, with his man on him again.

21. Even betting—Lilly freshning—both came up free. McCoy commenced by delivering a a tremendous blow on Lilly's mouth, starting the blood as from his own in the round before; clinch, and in falling, McCoy turned under, and Lilly fell in his lap.

22. McCoy came up smiling, with the blood streaming over his breast and upper lip, his left cheek and eye showing the effects of their heavy visitations.

He caught two sharp ones again on the old places, and in attempting to return, slipped and fell.

23 McCoy came up again; on approaching Lilly, he said in an under tone—"I've got you, sure enough!" which Lilly answered instanter, with a sharp cutting blow on the offending organ. McCoy rushed wildly in, when Lilly tapped him again, and in the clinch that followed, after some sharp in-fighting by both, Lilly was thrown.

24. Three or four sharp blows by Lilly in McCoy's dial;—all the round his, except the throw, which resulted in his going outside the ropes. Cheers for "Tom!"

25. Both cautious and self-possessed. Lilly stopped two mischievous looking offers, and in a clinch, threw his opponent heavily—falling on him.

26. McCoy, from the profuse manner in which he perspired—globules of sweat clustering all over the surface of his body—now plainly showed that his condition had been too fine; and to make the matter worse, his second (he could be said to have but one) after dragging him by the armpits to his corner, checked the glow by drenching with cold water. On coming up, he received a head hit which he countered in the breast heavily, then clinched his man, and threw him through the ropes.

27. Two sharp ones for Lilly in the old place—close, and both down. Even betting.

28. Lilly cool as a cucumber, and wary as an Indian—McCoy, on the contrary, too free, and too ready to fight. (Strange that his seconds could not tell him to restrain his ardor.) Lilly put in three successive terrific neck blows, which had a squelching sound that could be heard all over the crowd. McCoy, game as a pebble, and fearless as a lion, rushed wildly in, caught two or three more before he could clinch, and then was badly thrown.

29. McCoy's lip very much swollen, and the blood from his mouth streaming profusely over his breast. He appeared somewhat confused from the punishment of the former round, and received three successive hits in the face; the last carrying him down straight.

30. McCoy plainly showing his punishment, and his right eye also beginning to complain, while Lilly, save by a slight swelling of the upper lip, was scarcely marked. McCoy caught it again twice, and went down with the last blow clean.

31. McCoy evidently much fatigued and worried, caught it again severely in the old place—returned with a body blow, and dropped stupidly. Cries of " Go it, flower, you've got him licked now !"

32. Lilly had now proved himself by all odds the best hitter, and was also peculiarly adroit in saving himself from punishment and over-labor ;—on the other hand, McCoy was free and unguarded, and continually wasted himself with ineffectual efforts, in his ambition to do too much. Lilly planted one on his nose, at which McCoy clinched, but was pressed to the ropes, and, after a short struggle, was badly thrown, Lilly falling on him bodily as before,—Mac complaining of " foul " as he went to his corner.

33. McCoy's lip dreadfully swollen, and the whole contour of his face altering its expression. He struck strongly out after stopping a blow, and fell down on his knee.

34. Lilly got in another of his cutting blows on the right cheek,—a close, and sharp in-fighting, and a bad fall for McCoy : Lilly on top as usual, and in obedience to Sullivan's cries of " Lie on him, Chris ! lie on him !" remained on the breast of his gasping enemy until lifted off. The fight had now lasted forty minutes.

35. McCoy came up smiling through all his gore, and renewed the common trick which he had practised in the few first rounds, of pointing in a bantering manner to his own face, as if to say, " Why don't you hit me there ?" Lilly obliged him at once by planting a wicked shot on his nose which McCoy answered by a sharp rally and a close, which resulted in Lilly's being thrown, and his head striking smartly against one of the posts.

36. Both cautious ; heavy body blow for McCoy, and a tremendous counter

for Lilly in his neck. McCoy returned, but not getting home, fell.

37. McCoy confused, and very much astray. Instead of looking at his man, I saw his eyes glance around the ring. However, he righted before his situation was discovered or taken advantage of, and stopped a dangerous approach ; he then replied with a good effort, but not getting in, fell back from Lilly's threatened return.

38. Lilly got in another in the old place ; McCoy slightly answered it in the body, and went down.

39. Lilly waited for the assault, and kept well on his guard; McCoy, as usual led off, was stopped, and received a severe blow on his chin, followed by another on the right cheek ; McCoy then rallied, and rushed in, and they both dropped to the ground together ;—McCoy's arms being around Lilly's neck.

40. McCoy right at it again—struck a round blow which found its home on Lilly's left shoulder-blade ; endeavored to get in a repeater, but Lilly jumped quickly away, and he struck short, and fell—Lilly laughing.

41. McCoy stopped a mischievous offer from Lilly's left,---was not so fortunate in regard to his right, which caught him heavily in the breast,---McCoy rallied and was thrown hard---Lilly on top.

42. As McCoy came up, some one cried out " He's getting weak !" to which Tom replied, as he squared away, " I'm as strong as ever ;" and striking out as he spoke, caught Lilly with his right upon the breast, who tried to counter on the head, but didn't get in. Lilly then rushed in, and threw him heavily on his face, the blood gushing profusely from his mouth as he got up.

43. McCoy, notwithstanding his dreadful punishment, came up laughing, and was the first to begin Both hit together, after which they clinched, and Lilly fibbed him severely. A wrestle followed and McCoy was again badly thrown, with Lilly on him.

44. McCoy too ready, and worrying himself with unnecessary effort. He

made two or three lunges from which Lilly stepped lightly away. McCoy came up again, and while measuring for another blow, Lilly darted under his arm, rose behind, and let drive a tremendous shot on the left side of his head ; McCoy clinched, but was again badly thrown, with Lilly on him, though he managed to roll him over.

45. McCoy still bleeding profusely. On going up to the scratch, Sandford said to him, " Go at him now, as I told you Randall did, and you'll have him licked in three rounds !" to which Lilly scornfully replied, " I can lick him, and you after him, on the same afternoon." McCoy tolled him on by pointing at his face, which invitation was accepted by Lilly with two dreadful blows, one on the chin, and another death stroke on the neck. McCoy rushed in, returned it wildly on Lilly's head, and went down.

46. Light countering---Lilly cautiously approached, preparing for a fly, when McCoy dropped, and Lilly walked to his corner, laughing carelessly.

47. Light countering ; another sharp death blow in McCoy's neck ; a struggle, and he was heavily thrown.

48. Lilly got in four sharp successive hits, which spread the blood all over McCoy's face---he spat part of it back at Lilly, went in, and was again badly thrown. " $100 to 50 on Lilly"—taken by Sandford.

49. Heavy exchanges---rather in McCoy's favor, who drove Lilly to his own (Mac's) corner : where Lilly closed, and dropping his head, butted Mac in the stomach, throwing him back. Cries of " foul "---(long dispute, and "time " lost.)

50. On time being called, the men came up readily again. Counter hitting ---close, and McCoy heavily thrown, Lilly on top. (One hour.)

51. McCoy bleeding all the while, and his face disgustingly swollen and disfigured. Lilly hit him again on the mouth---closed---fibbed him severely--- threw him, and fell heavily upon him.

52. Two sharp hits on the head, and another death blow in the neck for Lilly, the last carrying McCoy down, clean.

53. Some cautious sparring---McCoy made a round hit in Lilly's back, and dropped away from the return.

54. In reply to some remark of Lilly's on their meeting at the scratch, McCoy replied---" Oh, there's no need of a hurry---we've got a week before us." Lilly waited for him, watched his chance, and dropped one on his old place on the mouth. McCoy quickly countered, and heavy lunges were exchanged, concluding with a splendid hit for McCoy on Lilly's chin ; the latter then rushed in, and after a mutual effort to fib, McCoy broke away and gave him the upper cut. Lilly rushed in again, when McCoy, summoning all his energies, made a desperate exertion, cross-buttocked him in fine style, and tossed him fairly on his head. ("Beautiful !" Great cheering for McCoy. " $100 on McCoy !")

55. Beautiful fighting again. McCoy freshening, though his countenance was horribly disfigured, and the blood still flowing quite free. Splendid hits for both----clinch---fierce struggle---Lilly thrown.

56. Counter---close---McCoy thrown, but turned Lilly outside the ropes.

57. A head hit for Lilly---McCoy returned, fell short, and dropped.

58. Wary figuring at the scratch---as McCoy was measuring for a fly, Lilly dropped his head, dodged under his arm, and clasping him about the waist, chopped him severely in the loins. McCoy writhed, however, from his disadvantage, and threw Lilly, who turned him as usual on their way to the ground, and fell on him.

59. McCoy's eyes in funeral black, and his mouth and throat full of blood, part of which he spat on Lilly's breast. Three successive equal counter hits; McCoy hit out again, but falling short, dropped.

60. Lilly stopped a well meant head blow, and in answer chopped McCoy downwards on his left cheek. Counter hits---close, and McCoy thrown badly.

61. Good body hit for McCoy---Lilly closed, caught McCoy by the legs, and threw him badly.

62. McCoy too ready, and wasting his strength by ineffectual efforts, while Lilly cautiously saved himself, McCoy stopped two dangerous offers beautifully.

and made another powerful lunge, but wide astray again. Lilly remained very cool, got in another stinging death blow on the neck, and followed it by three more in the face---a rush by Mc-Coy, in which he was thrown.

63. McCoy's seconds *at last* directed him not to fight so much. While he was sparring *away*, Lilly chopped him on the head by a downright blow---McCoy countered well on Lilly's mouth, and after receiving two more of the fatal neck blows, rushed in, and was badly thrown, the blood streaming from his mouth.

64. McCoy came up saturated to his very shoes with the cold water with which he was deluged every round, while Lilly was kept nearly dry. Lilly chopped him on the eye again, nearly closing it up---a close, and McCoy badly thrown, the blood gushing from his mouth again.

65. Both reeking with sweat. McCoy working too free again, and wasting powder in his heavy, useless lungs. Hit for Lilly on the right cheek, returned with interest by McCoy in a body blow, which carried Lilly down, clean.

66. After some figuring, Lilly got behind McCoy, clasped him round the waist, and letting him go, hit him as he fell. McCoy down.

67. Lilly caught him a dreadful blow on the cheek, which McCoy wildly returned, and was thrown, with Lilly on him.

68. Lilly scarcely hurt; McCoy failing fast. Counter hits, McCoy thrown as before.

69. Cries of " shutters up ? There's a death in the family !" &c. Two or three ineffectual lunges were made by McCoy, which only served to strain and weaken him; rush by Lilly, close, and Lilly thrown head first.

70. McCoy was now indeed a most unseemly object; both his eyes were black, the left one nearly closed, and indeed that whole cheek presented a shocking appearance. His very forehead was black and blue; his lips were swollen to an incredible size, and the blood streamed profusely down his chest. My heart sickened at the sorry sight. When he came up he appeared very weak, and almost gasping for breath, and endeavored while squaring away, to eject the clotting fluid from his throat. Several, who, like myself, compassionated the poor fellow's condition, cried, " Oh, take him away ! Take him away !" After getting a severe hit on the mouth, he rushed bravely in, closed, was thrown, but turned his opponent on the ground.

71. Rally, close; McCoy thrown, and Lilly down on him, heavy.

72. Heavy counter, three more sharp, deathly, neck blows for Lilly, a clinch, and McCoy thrown heavily, gasping under Lilly's weight.

73. McCoy's left daylight almost closed. Both cautious and fatigued. Hit and hit equal, clinch --McCoy caught Lilly's hair, and after working it backwards and forwards twice or thrice, bent him by main strength to the earth.

74. McCoy lunging in the air again--- Lilly carefully saving himself---McCoy rushed in, their hands became locked, and both fell side by side, Lilly exclaiming, with a laugh, as he rose, " By —— he's as weak as a rat."

75. Counter, in favor of McCoy--- close, fibbing by both; and McCoy badly thrown.

76. The sun appeared now to have a painful effect on McCoy's nearly closed optics. The eyelids were so swollen and stiff, with extravasated blood, that he was obliged to throw his head back, and expose his neck to his enemy, to enable him to look through the slight crevice left ; and this too in the seventy-sixth round. It was now perfectly apparent to every one present that poor McCoy had not the slightest chance to worst his cunning and active adversary. Blow after blow came raining in upon him, drawing blood, or threatening death at every stroke, and when he would seek to return, his antagonist would step lightly away, and his blow, wasted upon the trenchant air, had no other effect but that of wasting his strength. McCoy commenced again striking at random, received two stinging blows on the lip as admonishers---a close and was heavily thrown, Lilly on him.

77. Tom freshening wonderfully, got

in a good hit---counter---another good hit for Tom, and Lilly down on his knees.

78. Lilly showing great fatigue---McCoy went right to work, rallied, hit all over, clinched and threw Lilly heavily ---cheers. "$100 even on McCoy."

79. McCoy acting well, got in a terrific body blow, and a blow on the cheek ---a clinch and Lilly thrown.

80 Two heavy body hits for McCoy, rally by Lilly, counter, clinch at the ropes, and McCoy thrown heavily.

81. Lilly bettering, went right to work, put it into McCoy right and left, closed, and threw him heavily, falling on him.

82. McCoy came up unsteady, clinch, and McCoy thrown in the old way.

83. Counter, close, McCoy wooled Lilly, but was heavily thrown.

84. McCoy quite groggy, but still preserving the dignity of unflinching resolution in his gait. Lilly got in three severe hits, which McCoy returned open handed, a fatal sign-- clinch, and McCoy again badly thrown, Lilly falling on him.

85. As McCoy came up and made a pass, Lilly threw it aside, exclaiming, " O la !" then after making two splendid hits, rushed in and threw him heavily. On Lilly going to his corner, Sullivan kissed him, in admiration of his prowess.

86. McCoy bleeding and sweating profusely. Clinch---McCoy while twisting him to the earth by main strength, got him locked, then suddenly let go, giving him the upper cut as he sank, and raising a " mouse" on his left cheek with the blow.

87. Trifling counters, McCoy then struck out, overreached and weakly fell.

88. Though McCoy was now well nigh blinded, he came up well, led off and got in a pretty good body hit. Lilly answered sharp, clinched and threw him heavily and fell upon him, the blood gushing from McCoy's mouth, as he lay. Loud cries of " Shame, shame ! It's a shame to see such a game man beat to death !" The fight had now lasted two hours.

89. On bringing McCoy up, Ford and Sullivan cried out, " Oh take that man away. What's the use of beating him to death ? He can't win." Don't fret yourselves," replied Shanfroid, " he's got three hours fight in him yet. He's only beginning to work." " Finish him, then, Cris," returned Sullivan. Lilly let fly at the word, catching McCoy on the mouth, sending the blood in a fine spray in the sun---a rush by McCoy and Lilly thrown.

90. Lilly made two severe hits, close, McCoy pressed to the ropes and severely chopped.

91. McCoy very groggy, rushed in, wild, striking open handed---Lilly gave him two sharp cuts in the face, closed, and threw him dreadfully. Cries of " Take him away ! Don't let him fight any more !"

92. Blood spouting from McCoy's nose ; but he, still, nothing daunted--- clinch and both down.

93. Rally, close----Lilly chopped him severely in the loins, then threw him heavily and fell on him. As he was lifted up, Lilly looked down at him and exclaimed, " Be —— he's game ?" " 2 to 1 on Lilly."

94. As McCoy made a pass, Lilly dodged under his arm, caught him round the waist and chopped him badly on the back. While at it, McCoy dropped hopelessly in his arms, Lilly shoving him down and walking away. Cries of " it's a d—d shame to see a brave man used so !" " For God's sake take him away !"

95. McCoy came up unsteady, but stern and erect. Counter, close, both locked on the ropes---violent struggle, which ended in McCoy's receiving dreadful punishment, and a terrific fall with Lilly on him.

96. After a pass, Cris rushed in and threw McCoy in the old way.

97. McCoy staggering and gasping for breath ; Lilly hit him full in the mouth, when he turned around crazily and fell.

98. Sharp hit for Lilly ; McCoy dropped weakly from a repeater.

99. McCoy ready, though very weak ---a clinch and Lilly thrown.

100. McCoy came up well, counter, clinch, and they caught each other's hands. While in this position ; they turned, looked at each other, and ex-

changed a word ; then McCoy changed his hold, and · threw him by main strength, nearly on his head. Two hours and 16 minutes.

101. Lilly caught McCoy's head under his arm, jobbed him severely, and fell heavily upon him.

102. Close, sharp fibbing by both, struggle and both down ; Lilly spoke to McCoy in a low tone, as they lay on the ground together.

103. McCoy suffering very much, scarcely able to breathe, and spitting from his mouth solid clots and long strings of coagulated blood. He came up bravely (the noble boy !) without the slighest indication of a desire to shrink, got in a good body blow, but in the close was badly thrown.

104. McCoy got up himself at the cry of " time," astonishing every one by his wonderful endurance. Both his eyes were almost closed, and resembled purple cushions with a black cord drawn tightly through the middle, to represent the crevice through which he saw. He might be said to grope his way to the scratch. Lilly got in two light head blows, but in the clinch was thrown by a pure exertion of strength on the part of McCoy.

105. Smart counter---a close and both down, Lilly under---McCoy still strong.

106. McCoy rushed in as Lilly was preparing to strike and threw him.

107. McCoy came up slow, sticking his swollen tongue out and opening his mouth to get air, as if laboring under the sense of strangulation—

"And though his manly heart around,
No active currents warmly bound ;
Tho' swelled to bursting every vein,
No token gave he yet of pain."

As he stepped slowly up, Lilly cried out to him to come over to his side, upon which, Ford seeing his condition, exclaimed "Cris, now you've got him, sure !" " Not so sure as you imagine," immediately said the noble fellow, but in a voice so changed, so husky from its passage through the red current that was hemming out his life, that our very flesh crept as we heard it. His enemy could do as he pleased ; he hit him with impunity ; then rushed in and fell heavily upon him. He was " valiant no longer." The " puniest whisper"

might have "bearded" him without dread of harm.

108. The same—and McCoy thrown as before. Cries of "Take him out !"

109. Lilly put in three more short head blows, and threw him again with the same result. Time 2½ hours.

110. Cris rushed in—McCoy caught him by the hair and endeavored to fib him—failed, and was thrown hard.

111. McCoy very groggy, but still striking out strong. At the mark, while squaring he exclaimed, "I feel like a book !" As if unconscious where he was, however, he suddenly dropped his arms, and on the instant received a planter on the mouth and was severely thrown.

112. McCoy staggering in, but erect and dignified in his manner. Lilly planted another in the old place, starting the blood afresh—close, and McCoy down again, bad as ever. Ford here demanded that the brave fellow should be taken out, amid numerous cries of "Shame," and remarked that "Their doctor would be hung if they didn't." The latter branch of this remark was applied to a wretch who, from the fact of representing himself as physician, had been employed by the seconds of McCoy, for the express purpose of watching over the man's life, and of saving him, when his powers had been stretched to their extent of endurance. To him I chiefly lay the blame of Thos. McCoy's death, and as I presume there is a very general desire to bring him to justice, I will describe him at length. He is a tall, meagre, rickety, slabsided personage, with a shock of stiff, dirty hair, of a dusting brush grey, and a head so laterally compressed, as to present but the edge of a shingle for a face. His nose takes a start from a pair of inexpressive milky eyes, that could no more enliven his countenance, than could two brass nails irradiate a sweep s, and taking a bold curvilinear compass, juts out to an equal distance with a large knot or apple in his dirty scraggy neck. His shoulders are of an unequal height; the hollow which should adorn his back, is represented by a huge cavity in his belly, and he is altogether so pitiful a fellow, that I would blush at

my awkwardness if unable to cut a better "from a cheese paring after dinner."

113. Sharp body blow for Lilly—he then rushed in and endeavored to throw his opponent, but fell with the effort.

114. McCoy attended by his second up to the scratch. On being left to himself, he received two bad ones in the old places, and both fell.

115. McCoy completely in the dark. He made three good attempts to get in, and in the last fell with the effort.

116. McCoy led up again—caught a severe blow in the mouth, rushed in and was very badly thrown, having pitched head foremost at the ground and scraped his face along it for twelve or eighteen inches, before the impetus of his motion stopped.

117. Poor Tom failing fast—Lilly hit him a severe blow in the old place. McCoy obeying his instinct, rushed in, and by an exertion of latent strength, that astonished all, threw Lilly and fell upon him. Good, for a dying man! As he lay there, he patted his antagonist on his head, and smiled over him, as if this trifling fortune were amends. On being carried to his corner, he said to his seconds, "Nurse me—nurse me and. I'll whip him yet."

118. McCoy rushed wildly in, received a hit and a fall with Lilly on him that fairly shook the ground. Cries of "Shame! shame!" "For God's sake, save his life!" I did not hear that *the Doctor* interfered.

119. McCoy still indomitably game, came up perfectly blind, and took his position as erect as ever, and put out his arms mechanically. Shanfroid in reply to a rebuke for allowing such a man to fight longer, said "he ain't half licked yet!" Lilly rushed in and threw him, badly, falling on him as always before.

120. McCoy was lifted up heavily from his second's knee, and stood on his feet for the last time. He was led slowly to the mark, and took his position---a dying man---but as erect, as dignified, as game as ever. Lilly was also much fatigued, and enduring considerable suffering from the heavy body blows he had received. They both sparred cautiously; McCoy leading off,

as ever, and making two or three good efforts to get in without success. Lilly then rushed in, closed and threw him very hard, fell with his whole weight upon him, and remained upon the dying man until lifted off. On approaching him (McCoy) he was found to be perfectly inanimate, and sank lifeless in his second's arms. Time was called, but not, alas.! for him. Poor fellow, he was doomed never to hear sound again, till the challenge of the last trumpet shall pierce the portals of his ears, and summon him, with those who did foul murder on him, to a *mark* from which there can be no dodging—no escape.

He had fought for *two hours and forty three minutes*, receiving eighty-one heavy falls, with his antagonist on him, and bleeding, certainly, for two and a half hours. He fought with good heart, but not well; showing by his open motions everything that he was about to do, and fighting too much. He had also suffered, no doubt, from over training, having previous to the match been in very ill health.

As soon as he had been declared the victor, Lilly jumped up, slapped his hands with an exclamation of joy, and then amid the cheers of his circle, sprang over the ropes of the ring. He was but little marked, and not severely hurt. Poor McCoy, on being lifted from the ground, sank as limp as a rag in his second's arms. A cry was made for the Doctor, and a movement in the mass took place to give him air. I forced my way in the crowd and took a look at the dying man. God grant that I may never see such another sight! He lay upon his back, his face and neck one bruised, unseemly, bloated mass of incipient corruption; gasping for breath, and sucking by the violence of his raspiration, his bloated lips far back in his mouth. In the next moment he ceased to breathe, and word went in a hoarse whisper that *he was dead!* Never shall I forget the talismanic horror of that expression. The cheeks of old and young, the fledging villian, and the ruffin stepped in crime, all blanched to ashes, and exchanging a look of vague and undefined fear, separated silently, and sought their respective boats. Not a loud sound or rough expression was heard by the vast assemblage that collected at the landing. Solemnly each man embarded, and silently east off and bore away. I went in the dead man's boat, and sailed back with him, lying, stark, currupt and dead, in the same cabin, where he in the morning lay full of life, health, hope, strength, and manhood. I leave the moral with the reader.

REPORT OF THE BATTLE

BETWEEN

GEORGE KENSETT AND NED HAMMOND,

For $500 a Side—December 7, 1826.

At the solicitation of a large number of our readers we below give a report of the fight between George Kensett and Ned Hammond which took place on the 7th of December, 1826. We are indebted to a friend, who kindly loaned us a little pamphlet containing an account of the battle. It appears to be a report gotten up by a friend of one of the parties. However, we give word for word, that our readers may see how such things were done in former days :

In giving the history of a contest or combat between two men, I am aware of the risk I run of offending the feelings of many a canting, whining swindler and fastidious hypocrite, who will shake the head of disapprobation at the name of a fight, and fleece you at the same instant. I know I shall commit great violence upon these shadows of morality, who so much infest the world, who have the impudence to hold themselves up as our judges and superiors, entitling themselves to great respect—constantly assuming a solemn gravity before the world, to cover their own ignorance or crafty designs ; who condemn in others, what they practice without scruple. To such, the following remarks are not directed ; my whole object is, to disclose plain facts, undisguised, and being unconnected or influenced by either of the combatants—I shall endeavor to give a candid and disinterested description of the whole affair. I am compelled to make one sweeping observation, viz : That many persons upon this occasion violated every principle of justice and moderation—the result of the contest, or rather the scandalous and unsatisfactory decision given by careless or interested umpires, will remain a stain upon the character of those who meanly or tamely acquiesced in so gross and palpable an imposition. In this strange farce we find Patrick Burns, an umpire, triumphantly giving the victory to his countryman, when he was unable to rise from his second's knee, or approach the scratch, while Kensett was perfectly fresh and unhurt ; these proceedings were all a perfect burlesque—then to witness Fuller, giving up Sutton's stakes of $100, in such a hurry ; he must have been stultified. It looks like a compound system of juggling throughout, as the description of the fight will more clearly point out. In order to enlist the feelings of the ignorant in the favor of Hammond, this party fabricated and gave circulation to a falsehood, which hundreds can contradict ; they pretended that Kensett forced Hammond into this contest, when it is well known that Hammond challenged Kensett twice publicly, and even had the daring at the same time to include any man in America, within a few pounds of his own weight. There is now no fear of a recurrence of such empty blustering, as Hammond is well convinced by the helpless situation to which he was reduced, in the late fight, that he has no chance with such a customer, except by foul play, or the same precious umpires. I speak in strict justice to Hammond, that he entered the ring with as much confidence as Kensett, but soon discovered his inferiority in the sharp conflict ; he often had recourse to a deliberate method of falling on Kensett's body, with his hip ; which although observed by the umpires, and known to be unfair, yet it was passed by unnoticed ; after these few introductory remarks, I shall proceed to describe the particulars.

A match was made between Kensett and Hammond, to have a fair stand-up fight for five hundred dollars aside, and the 7th day of December was fixed upon for the struggle, within fifty miles of the city of New York, in a twenty-four foot ring ; half minute time—one thousand dollars were entrusted with Mr Sweeney, to place in the hands of P. G. Hart, as the stakeholder ; a short time previous to the day of meeting, there was a verbal agreement between the contending parties, to carry the spectators to the scene of action, at the same price ; but the object of the Hammondites was to fill their vessel with friends, at any rate, nor were they particular about their customers, so long as they were partizans ; and were acquainted with the countersign, or signal. It's true, some persons of respectability found their way on board, by mistake, nor did they discover their error until they found themselves surrounded by the rabble ; on reaching the place of destination, and the umpires were about to be appointed, Englishmen were objected to, but they fully approved of Patrick Burns, who had bets pending in favor of Hammond, and which according to the laws of fighting amounts to a disqualification, and his acceptance of the office, under these glaring circumstances, and what followed, will naturally suggest in the minds of fair men something highly unfavorable, and which cannot easily be removed. A gentleman, although a novice, was chosen to act with Burns, under the superintendence of Fuller, who promised his advice and instruction ; he declined being a principal, in consequence of being attacked for being a pugilist,

but all that we know upon this head is, that he suffered a critical question to be decided in ignorance, in direct opposition to his own judgment, upon which thousands of dollars, and other very material and important points depended. This mysterious business will require more explanation than has yet been given. The referee was smuggled away by artifice, of which fact Kensett and his friends were totally ignorant. Varions attempts were made to create confusion in favor of Hammond, and the ring was broken in for this purpose; even Mr. Fuller expressed his astonishment and indignation at such an outrage, and publicly declared that everything on the part of Kensett was fair and honorable ; and in a few minutes after, to the amazement of every gentleman on the ground, unjustly gave up the one hundred dollars of Sutton's money, without any hesitation, and while under a full conviction himself, at the moment that the umpires decided in error. The public wish to learn from Mr. Fuller, what motive influenced him on this occasion ; whether it was a pusillanimous fear, or did he court the favor and patronage of the Irish. I proceed to Peter G. Hart, the stakeholder, who was notified not to give up Kensett's money ; but he justifies himself in so doing, by stating that he gave it back to the person of whom he received it, without waiting for, or receiving any instruction from the umpires ; and Sweeney without any hesitation gave the same up to Hammond, although otherwise instructed. Sweeney gave his word of honor to hold back the stakes until the dispute was decided.

THE BATTLE.

First round. Both men when stripped looked in the best possible condition, each second betted on his man, and being brought to the scratch and giving the usual shake of the hand, both retreated a little and the fight commenced. Hammond struck right and left, which took no effect ; Kensett very cool and mischievous in his hitting. Hammond got the fall.

2. In this round Hammond gave Kensett a good blow on the side, which

caused Kensett to throw several good hits away; Hammond fighting with courage and resolution. Kensett made some fine counter hits—stops, and returned with the rapidity of lightning, leaving visible marks of a finished workman---in a close Kensett weaving in great style---both fell on their sides--- Hammond rolled over upon Kensett.

3. Both men blowing a little---Kensett took the lead, Hammond fighting bravely---though he was bleeding very profusely---a slight tincture of claret from the bottom of Kensett's left ear--- Kensett gave Hammond a flush hit in the face as he was rushing in, which sent him a great distance, and dropped him as if shot from a rifle---the blow was heard all round the ring---this evidently secured the fight to Kensett--- who nodded his head at him and smiled, implying that Hammond must be a good man if he could win the fight after that.

4. Hammond appeared very much distressed---piping. Kensett had reco-covered his first wind---Kensett continued to give two blows to his one, all telling upon poor Hammond's day lights ---in a close, Kensett again heavily weaving, both down, Hammond uppermost.

5. Hammond appeared at the scratch very groggy---in this round Hammond took a great deal, and gave but little, it was all Wall street to a bushel of murphies in favor of Kensett---in closing both fell upon their sides.

6. Kensett looked fresh, cool and steady—the fire of Hammond's courage was gone—his head in Chancery—his window shutters were up—his face and body drenched in claret, he was a most piteous object—Kensett gave him five blows without one being returned— Hammond tried to grip him—Kensett fell from between his arms exhausted from the force of his own hitting---and Hammond fell upon him. At this point of the battle a bull jumped into the ring, vociferating that Hammond had won the fight---at the same time throw-ing up his hat as the signal for victory. The seconds quickly expelled this fellow.

7. With great difficulty Hammond was raised from his bottle-holder's knee, and while the second was fruitlessly attempting to bring him to the scratch--- Sandford, the bottle-holder of Hammond ---run eagerly to Burns, the umpire on the other side---*saying*, dont you think Kensett fell without a blow in the last round? At this hint---Burns instantly jumps up and exclaims--By Jasus he did !---then putting up both his arms— which evidently appears to have been a previously concerted signal for breaking into the ring ;—you therefore perceive, that at the time they were perfectly convinced that their man was completely beaten they then had recourse to stratagem. When they discovered Hammond was beat, the whole motley group forced themselves into and about the ring, with the greatest violence—they set up a yell equal to the most savage tribe of Indians---bearing Hammond away from the ground, calling him victor, and this outrageous turbulence was continued into the very streets of New York.

They created *a wrangle* respecting Kensett's falling, after finishing a long rally, although Hammond fell flat at the same time—which removed all quibbles about its being foul. A fair stand-up fight signifies that a man is not to strike and then drop wilfully---but where two men close, then either may get out of the clutches of the other in the best way he finds a chance ; but is not compelled to allow the other to fall upon him when he can in any way avoid it ; under such circumstances, and every rule of fighting (in the London ring) the man who keeps his post longest wins the battle ; of course leaving the ring before the dispute is settled---loses it.

Kensett offered to put up $1,000 against the $1,000 stake money which had been fought for, and fight Hammond at any time he chose, but to this the opposite party would not agree.

REPORT OF THE LATE FIGHT

Alfred Walker and Joe Hoiles, the Spider,

FOR ONE HUNDRED POUNDS A SIDE AND THE FEATHER WEIGHT CHAMPIONSHIP.

From Bell's Life in London, April 16.

In our last we acquainted our readers with the preliminary arrangements that had been made for this Championship battle in miniature, and we now, in accordance with a promise made in the same paper, proceed to lay before the public the details of the affair subsequent to the publication of our journal, premising that the mill excited quite as much interest among the *cognoscenti* as the battle for the Championship between the rival Harrie's (Broome and Orme) which took place about the same time last year.

It will be remembered that the fixture for the sealing was the Duke of Argyll, Laystall street, Liquorpond-street, the *hostelrie* of Alfred Walker, and thither, between the hours of twelve and two o'clock, on Monday, a very numerous assemblage of the lovers of pugilism directed their steps, and we should say that, after the mill, when Master Alfred returned to the bosom of his family, from which he had been so long estranged, his buxom better half was enabled to render him such an account of the receipts over the bar, as would induce him to exclaim, with the Highlanders of old, " God bless the Duke of Argyll." The Spider, our readers are aware, was confined to 7st. 11lb., and on that amount of dead weight being deposited in the scale, he took his seat on the machine, but the beam did not move—thus proving that he was far below the stipulated amount; in fact, we are informed by his trainer that he did not in reality exceed 7st. 4½lb. He looked well and confident, and offers were made to back him at 6 to 4. Walker, who was confined to 8st. 4lb., was also well within the prescribed 116lb.,

as he did not weigh above 7st. 12lb. He, like his Arachnidæan adversary, was confidence itself; he looked pale, but was evidently in excellent health. He was not blessed with a very large supply of the rowdy, and, consequently, was unable to make any considerable outlay on the result of the battle. In the course of the evening, both the bantams showed at Johnny Walker's benefit, at Saville House, and were loudly cheered. An early adjournment to roost took place, and on the eventful morning they were astir betimes.

Long before eight o'clock the bustle in the neighborhood of Shoreditch betokened the excitement that was abroad respecting the affair ; and as that hour drew near, the rush of cabs, Hansom and otherwise, filled with well-known ring-goers, proved that the attendance would be both numerous and respectable. This, however, we had fully anticipated ; we knew that the Rising Sun, in Air street, had been crowded the previous evening with the tip-top patrons of milling, and that a large and select party of Corinthians had congregated at another celebrated house of resort for " millers" in a more westerly and aristocratic part of the town, where, after a gorgeous spread, they had discussed the battles of ancient times, and had speculated to a considerable amount upon the combat now under notice, many bets being laid about the " double event," 5 to 1 being freely offered and taken about the two Walkers winning their battles. The waiters at this celebrated crib were compelled to be early astir, as the intended travelers, who had not been present at a mill since the advent of Mr. Pinxtone, as caterer-general, were not aware of the change for the better which had taken place in the grubbery department, and, therefore, warned by experience, they, determined to lay in such a supply of belly timber as would, if necessary, last them until their return to the metropolis. And now, " to return to our muttons." The cabs, as we were observing, poured into the yard at Shoreditch station in quick succession, and many were the familiar faces that we recognised, which are seldom met with at a mill unless it be one of paramount interest By the time for starting there could not have been less than 100 Corinthians of the highest order, and a proportionate number of other ring-goers of humbler order being added, the crowd upon the platform was something considerable. The only absentee of any great note was his reverence of Bond street, but that worthy has of late so neglected his flock that his non-attendance at a mill is looked upon rather as a matter of course. A special train had been chartered for the occasion by Alec Keene and Johnny Walker, and, judging from appearances, they must have reaped an abundant harvest. A saloon carriage was attached for the use of the Patricians, but, as this would only hold 25 or 30, many, of course, were compelled to resort to the ordinary first-class carriages. In the saloon, however, were to be found most of the regular frequenters of the P. R., and among them a good deal of money was speculated on the way down. Bets were laid on double and treble events. In some instances money was laid out on the Spider—his name being coupled with King Tom for the Derby—in other cases Autocrat and the Spider was backed. When the event of the day only was touched upon, the prices varied considerably, throughout the morning. The first bet we heard laid was 18 to 12 on Spider, afterwards we heard 14 to 8, 20 to 10, &c. The train, which did not leave Shoreditch until half-past eight, proceeded but slowly to Chesterford, where an old patron of the sport was taken up, and final orders were given to the engineer, who then mended his pace, but the *tocus in quo* was not reached until near twelve o'clock. Here a kind friend and patron was in waiting

to act as pilot, and a move was quickly made to the scene of action. We regret to state that, during the process of debarkation, some of those gentry, who have no respect for the laws of *meum and tuum*, and who we were in hopes had long ago determined to " drop the shop," when out on a pleasure excursion, so far forgot themselves as to borrow a ticker, the property of a gentleman, who kindly granted the use of his lands for the mill. So poor a return for his hospitality could not, of course, be allowed ; and, through the exertions of Alec Keene the watch was returned, on payment of a couple of sovereigns out of the funds of the Pugilistic Association. For the information of the conveyancers in question, we may just hint that no such reward will, in future, be paid them, and it will therefore be as well if they confine their practice to the metropolis, otherwise it will be found necessary to adopt some means to prevent their attendance at a sport which we believe to be as much a favorite with them as with other ring-goers. " A nod is as good as a wink to a blind horse," and we trust that our nimble-fingered friends will take our hint in the kindly spirit in which it is meant.

As soon as an eligible piece of ground had been selected, Tom Oliver, assisted by Tom Callas and others, set to work with alacrity, and fixed the ropes and stakes on an excellent piece of turf. The inner and outer rings were arranged, and the sale of tickets for the former was carried on with great rapidity, and by the commencement of the fight no less than £24 17s. 6d. had been realised. Massey, who made his first appearance in the character of Inspector of Ring Police, rallied his forces round him, and cleared the arena for action in a way that did him infinite credit, and we may as well state at once that the ring was preserved from first to last most admirably.. The Spider was the first to appear at the ring side, and it was some twenty minutes before he was followed by his opponent. Meantime, the little fellow busied himself by disposing of his colors, in which, we believe, he was eminently successful. He was attended by that prince of seconds Jack

Macdonald, and Billy Hayes, who had come specially from his training quarters for the purpose, and who looked as fresh as paint. By one o'clock Walker, accompanied by his brother Johnny and his seconds, Jerry Noon and George Brown, made his appearance, and the diminutive champions at once stepped within the arena, where they shook hands in a most friendly way, and proceeded at once to arrange the preliminaries. The toss for choice of corners was won by Keene on behalf of the Spider, who of course placed his opponent with his face to the sun, and in a corner rather lower than his own. A referee was then chosen, and the Spider having tried in vain to lay out a £50 note, at 50 to 30, they commenced their toilettes under a blazing sun, from which, however, they were partially defended by gigantic umbrellas of the Gamp pattern. While they are in the hands of their valets we will, according to custom, and by the desire of numerous readers, give such facts in connection with their former careers as are in our possession. Alfred Walker, who is about 26 years of age, and stands 5ft. 3in., is, as our readers know, the youngest brother of the renowned Johnny Walker, formerly champion of the light weights, and now again a candidate for the same office. Previous to his contest on Tuesday he had only twice essayed his powers in the P. R., first with Darby, of Walsall, a bigger and heavier man than himself, over whom he obtained a victory, after a long and determined contest, in which he had a very uphill game to play. His other battle was with Jack Hicks, and must be fresh in the recollection of our readers ; it took place Nov. 30, 1852, and lasted 2 hours and 45 minutes, ending in a draw on account of the darkness. Hicks was very much punished, and almost blind, while the hero of our tale, although his hands were both much injured, was otherwise comparatively unharmed, and, had there been a little more daylight, would, barring an accident, have come off a second time victorious ; as it was, however, the friends of both men, considering that they had done enough for money, would not permit them to meet

again, and presented to each the sum for which he had contended. Walker now retired into comparative quiet, and devoted himself to his business. There were several nibbles on his part at the Spider, but the latter declined to bite, deeming it unwise to give away the weight required by Walker, who would only consent to confine himself to 8st. 4lb., below which he doubted whether he could come. At length, however, the Spider, throwing aside all fear of the consequences, some time after his battle with Bowers, issued a challenge to fight any man in the world, and give half a stone, confining himself to 7st. 11lb ; and this challenge being taken up by Walker, the present match was made— a match, be it observed, which was looked upon by many as extremely injudicious on the part of the Spider, who, it was known, would not be much over 7st. 5lb., and, therefore, if his adversary was near the stipulated 8st. 4lb., would be giving nearly a stone—an advantage for which it was thought all the cleverness in the world could not compensate. A great " entomologist," however, and staunch admirer of the Spider, considered that if little Joey " fancied " a man, he would be very near licking him, whoever he might be, and promised him his support, and the match; which many imagined would end in a forfeit to Walker, proceeded. Master Alf. was therefore compelled to doff the apron, and betake himself with all speed to the flannels, in which, under the guidance of his able brother, Johnny, he got himself into such good condition on the Newmarket Downs as to justify the remark that he was fit to fight for his life. He is a civil, quiet, well-behaved young man, and is a general favorite.

The Spider, who is about 25 years of age, is a sprig from the Borough school, and is far better known in the pugilistic world than his opponent. He commenced his career March 28th, 1848, with one Cornwell, for £10 a side, when he obtained an easy victory in 18 rounds, and 29 minutes. He next fought and beat Jemmy Herbert for £25 a side, in in 100 rounds, occupying two hours and fifteen minutes, Jan. 29th, 1850. On

Sept. 24th, the same year, he vanquished Jemmy Madden, after an exciting contest, in 56 rounds, and 91 minutes. After this, on the 14th of January, 1851, he fought a draw with Harry Adams, the battle ending, after two hours duration, in a disputed foul blow. In Sept. 1861, he fought and beat Jemmy Trainer, of Liverpool, for £50 a side, in 49 rounds, and 80 minutes; and, after this, we do not find him engaged in a pugilistic encounter until his battle with Bill Bowers of Billingsgate, on the 19th of April last year, when he gained rather an easy victory in 1h. 24min., during which 25 rounds were fought. The contest might, no doubt, have been prolonged had Bowers been gifted with a larger share of pluck, but we doubt whether the result could have been altered. The circumstances attending the present match have been alluded to in our short summary of the doings of Walker, and therefore require no further comment. The Spider, by his universal good conduct, has endeared himself to all who know him, while his trim, neat, little figure, and his extreme cleverness in the use of his feelers, have procured for him general admiration, and he is always looked upon as the wonder of the *feather* tribe. He took his final breathing for the contest of Sutton, where he was looked after by Billy Hayes, so that, by a singular coincidence the champion of the feather weights was trained by the champion of the light weights, while the candidate for honors among the feathers was looked after by the candidate for the light weight championship. And now, having exhausted all we have to say in the shape of introductory matter, we will to the description of the mill. All being in readiness, at 26 minutes after one, the youths were delivered at the scratch, the usual daddle shaking took place, and business commenced.

THE FIGHT.

Round 1. As soon as the men stood in battle array, all eyes, were of course, directed to their appearance. The Spider looked as graceful as ever, his neatly turned legs, small feet and ancles, immensely long arms and delicate wrists,

created much astonishment among those who had never seen him peeled; but, although there was a delicacy of form, there was also an appearance of that strength to be found in his namesake of the insect tribe. True, he was thin, and light looking, but there was plenty of muscle upon his feelers, and also on his back and shoulders, and his small snakelike head and neck gave him a sharp, wide awake appearance, which, coupled with a smile of easy confidence, increased the confidence of his friends, who were vociferous in their offers to back him 2 to 1—odds which the friends of Walker were not backward in accepting; in which we may say they were justified by the appearance of their champion. Walker stands about half an inch taller than the Spider, and, on throwing himself into attitude, displayed a muscular development which could hardly have been expected in so small a man. His figure reminded us strongly of his brother Johnny in his palmy days, broad shouldered, sturdy, and square. His arms were not so long as the Spider's, but they were far more muscular, and were evidently dangerous weapons when wielded by one said to possess equal skill with his brother in the art of hitting. His attitude was good, but to our mind too stiff; but this might have been in comparison to his opponent, who is remarkable for his easy, elegant position. He looked all the 7lb heavier than the Spider, and was evidently a dangerous customer, and one looked upon by many good judges (not led away by their blind confidence in the little one) as an almost certain conqueror. Little time was lost on either side in sparring; the Spider went at once to his man, feinted, and let go his left, which reached Alf's right brow rather heavily. The Spider grinned, and again put out his *antenna*, but Walker was prepared for him, and let go his left to counter him, and the Spider seeing this drew back his arm. The Spider made a second attempt of a like nature, which was foiled by Walker's sledge hammer. Joe then, as if tired of vain attempts, dashed in, and some slight exchanges took place, Walker on the ribs and the Spider on the right cheek; Walker's head at the same mo ment coming in contact with the stake. No great damage was done, and the Spider slipped down.

2. Walker, without any ado, opened the ball by dashing out his left and right; the former was short, but the latter reached Joe's left peeper. The Spider returned quickly on the left cheek and in getting away slipped and fell on his nether end. Walker also overreaching himself, fell.

3. Walker again commenced proceedings. as if determined to cut the Spider down at once. He caught the Spider on the left side of the head heavily with his left, and the Spider missed his return. Walker then closed, and some mutual fibbing, without mischief, took place, and Walker in the end finding he could not throw the Spider, got down, getting a rap from the Spider's left as he fell.

4. Walker again went in, and caught the Spider on the left cheek, the latter, however, countered him beautifully, on the mouth, a very straight hit, and drew *first blood.* Walker persevered——he dashed in, but in an ungraceful scrambling way, with his arms wide apart, and the insect shot out his left heavily on the dexter peeper, and then his right on the ribs. Walker missed with both hands. He tried again, but only reached the Spider's left shoulder with his right. Still he would not be denied, and as he went open armed at the Spider, the latter met him straight on the left eye, inflicting a cut from which the ruby was quickly perceptible, Walker reaching his ribs heavily with his right in return. A close at the ropes followed, in which Walker got the Spider round the waist, close to the corner stake, and pegged away heavily with his disengaged arm at the ribs, on which he left very visible marks of his knuckles. At length both fell over the ropes, Walker uppermost.

5. Walker's right cheek was a good deal swollen and his left eye showed the marks of the Spider's handy-work, being nearly closed. Offers of 3 and 4 to 1 on the Spider were now heard, and indeed seemed to be justified by the appearance of the men, the Spider being

as yet without a scratch, and both Walker's eyes showing evidence of going into mourning. Walker again went wildly in with his arms open, and let go both hands. The Spider cleverly stepped between them, however, and dashed out his nimble left, catching Alf very straight on the right cheek, and immediately got out of harm's way. Walker, who clearly had orders to force the fighting, and to go in at all hazards, followed him up, and the Spider, nothing loth, stood and hit with him. Walker's blows missed, while the little one propped him beautifully on the bridge of his conk, a regular stinger, and both were then down in a scramble, Spider undermost.

6. Walker, on the same system, went to work, and let go his left and right, but was beautifully stopped by the smiling Spider, who seemed to treat his efforts with contempt. He tried again, and once more did his smeller come in contact with the Spider's left feeler, which was sent out as straight as a carpenter's rule. The Spider then went at his opponent, and attempted to repeat the visitation, but Walker jumped away, and the Spider, overbalancing himself, fell flat on his face.

7. Walker as usual went in with both hands in a determined manner, but the Spider cleverly avoided both, and, with great quickness, planted his right on Alfred's left peeper, missing a visitation on the dial with his left. Walker then bored in, and closed, and both fell.

8. Walker, whose phisog was much flushed, came up laughing, as did his gallant little opponent, whose quickness and skill were universally admired. Walker let go both hands, but the Spider avoided his blows and planted his left on the bread basket. Walker again followed him up, and napped another tell-tale hit on the left ogle from the Spider's right. He succeeded, however, in planting a severe counter-hit on the mouth, which drew claret, and seemed almost to knock the Spider off his pins. It was evidently a hot one, but Joe treated it with contempt and closed. Walker almost succeeded in getting down, but the Spider cleverly lifted him up, and, after a long struggle succeeded in throwing, and falling on him.

9 and last. Walker went in as he had done in each of the previous rounds, and the Spider, nothing loth, went to him and attempted, as before, to prop him as he lunged out. He missed him, however, and Walker's blow, coming with great force, caught the poor little fellow on the left temple, and down he fell. It was at once seen that all was over. His seconds shook him, and threw water on him as he lay unconscious in the middle of the ring, but to no purpose. They then carried him to his corner, and after a copious sousing with water, he appeared slightly to recover. He was carried to the scratch, but on being put upright, was unable to stand; he staggered, and again falling forward, was caught by his seconds. It was, of course long after time, and Walker had by this time left the ring. Some of Spider's friends attempted to claim the fight on the ground that Walker had left the ring before time was called. We did not see when he left, our attention being directed to the Spider, but as the latter was clearly out of time, and unable to walk to the scratch, this was a mere quibble, which was no doubt suggested in the heat of the moment, and adopted by those who, like ourselves, could scarcely believe their eyes, and were loth to imagine it possible that the Spider was actually beaten in so short a time as *sixteen minutes and half.* Reflection and inquiry, however, convinced these parties that there was no justice in their claim, and it was not pursued. Walker was proclaimed the winner, amidst the cheers of his patrons, and all being over, a move in the direction of the train took place.

The Spider, on reaching his carriage, was much affected at his ill-fortune, but was somewhat consoled by the hope of better luck next time. Beyond a slight mark on the temple, and a cut on his upper lip, he had not a scratch, while Walker's right eye was nearly closed, the left not much better; his mug was considerably swollen, and strongly indicative of Joe's powers as a portrait painter. All the spectators, were, with some difficulty, got into the train, and the expedition got under way for home by half-past three o'clock, and, after a slow and tedious journey, the *voyageurs* were safely landed in the metropolis by half-past six. The only consolation for the shortness of the mill being that it was, so far as it went, a manly, straightforward affair—and was so far unsatisfactory in its result, that a second passage of arms between the same men must inevitably be the result.

REMARKS.

The short duration of this affair necessarily tends greatly to curtail our usual remarks. It was clear, from the very commencement, that the gallant little Spider held his opponent much too cheap, and was so eager to cut him down at once, that all regard for his own personal safety seemed to be thrown on one side. He apparently thought himself invulnerable and invincible, and forgetting that he was opposed to a stronger and better man than he had ever before met, went to work in his old style, and a very pretty and telling style it was, when played with caution. Each round evidently gave him fresh confidence; he was enabled to get on to Walker's dial heavily, and frequently with impunity, and succeeded in so damaging his optics, that one was completely closed on the following day, and the other was in deep mourning. He has, if possible, improved since he fought Bowers, and his extraordinary quickness and the length of his reach, coupled with his cool determination, completely electrified those who had never before seen him figure in the P. R. We should have been better pleased, however, to see a little more caution exhibited at the commencement. To attempt to cut down a formidable adversary like Walker was exceedingly bad generalship, and was contrary to the advice of his seconds and friends. Confidence is a very good thing, but when carried to excess often leads us into error. Had he kept away, and contented himself with a prop now and again, at long shots, instead of going to close quarters, the very game to suit such an adversary as Walker, he would have stood a much better chance of victory. He has no doubt learned a lesson on this occasion which will not, in future, be thrown away upon him.

THE GOOD TIME COMING.

RESPECTFULLY DEDICATED TO THE NEW-YORK FANCY.

BY FRANK QUEEN.

There's a good time coming, boys,
A good time coming :
"Old Fogies" now must all take heed
That the Sporting World will take the lead
In the good time coming :
Once they were looked upon as small,
But now they're growing stronger ;
And very soon they'll have *the call*—
Wait a little longer.

There's a good time coming, boys,
A good time coming :
A new *Race Course* is being made,
Where *heavy odds* will oft be laid
In the good time coming ;
Lecompte's *great time* must there be beat,
For Hiram's arms are stronger
To guide a nag in a *four mile heat*—
Wait a little longer.

There's a good time coming, boys,
A good time coming :
In *Yachting* there are rumors rife
Of Matches made for friendly strife,
In the good time coming :
The *Bianca* long has had the sway,
But they're building others stronger
In Philadelphia, so they say—
But, wait a little longer.

There's a good time coming, boys,
A good time coming :
Men who make a match to *Fight*,
Will take good care that *all is right*
In the good time coming ;
Shun all tricks and crosses too,
For honesty is stronger,
And holds all rascals up to view—
Wait a little longer.

There's a good time coming, boys,
A good time coming :
There's many *feats* we have in view,
Of *running, walking, leaping*, too,
In the good time coming.
With England's sons our own will try
Which of them is stronger :
We'll have rare matches by-and by—
Wait a little longer.

There's a good time coming, boys
A good time coming .
Canadians say New-York shall yield
When next they meet upon the *Field*,
In the good time coming.
But the *Cricketers* of New-York, state
Their arms are growing stronger,
To gain the prize their foes must wait—
Just a little longer.

There's a good time coming, boys,
A good time coming :
Henceforth all classes will resort
Where they can see the *best of sport*
In the good time coming ;
Treat all alike—act "on the square,"
The cause will soon grow stronger,
In view of this it is but fair—
To wait a little longer.

There's a good time coming, boys,
A good time coming :
The CLIPPER will her sails unfurl,
And bring us *news* from all the world
In the good time coming :
Those who can, will take the field
To make our *influence* stronger,
For the sporting cause must be upheld—
Wait a little longer.

THE FIGHT AT BOSTON CORNERS.

BY FRANK QUEEN.—*Air*—WAKE OF TEDDY THE TILER.

'Twas on the twelfth October last,
On Wednesday of the week just past,
When all the "Fancy" hurried fast,
 To the fight at Boston Corners.
Sullivan made a match to fight,
With a man named Morrissey, all so tight,
And said he'd spoil the Trojan's sight,
And bruise his head both left and right.
Yet Morrissey feared him not a bit ;
But said he'd give him hit for hit
And knock him in a fainting fit
 At the fight at Boston Corners.
  Helter, skelter, how they go,
  Slashing, crashing, twas'nt slow,
  'Twas jolly times I'd have you know
   At the fight at Boston Corners.

The ring was made on even ground,
And thousands thronged it all around ;
But a referee, long, could not be found
 For the fight at Boston Corners.
At last they found one who would do,
'Twas very near the hour of two,
And the people tired and hungry grew
When Morrissey's cap in the ring he threw.
Wilson soon did Yankee bring,
Who jumped the rope with nimble spring,
And landed in the inner ring,
 For the fight at Boston Corners.
  Helter, skelter, how they go, &c., &c.

"Time" was called ; to fight the match
The men both walked up to the "scratch"
When Morrissey's eye did a "peeler" catch
 At the fight at Boston corners.
He then dealt out some heavy blows,
Which reached the Yankees eyes and nose,
And brought him on his hands and toes,
While Morrissey's friends cried "there he
 goes."
Sullivan now began his "tricks"
By going down to escape the licks
Which came upon him thick as "bricks"
 At the fight at Boston Corners.
  Helter, skelter, &c., &c.

The fourth round was the hardest fought :
And both men numerous "rippers" caught,
Rather more than either saught
 At the fight at Boston Corners.
At round the fifth, they both fought shy :
But Sullivan let a "stinger" fly,
Which caught poor Morrissey on the eye,
When his seconds lanced it "on the sly !"
While his face and body dripped with gore,
Poor Morrissey, suffering, fought the more,
And knocked the Yankee on the floor,
 At the fight at Boston Corners.
  Helter, skelter, &c., &c.

The men both fought so very well,
Which had the best 'twas hard to tell ;
Till Morrissey's eye began to swell
 At the fight at Boston Corners.
And now the Yankee tried to prop

Game Morrissey in the "same old spot,"
Who found he couldn't stand the shock ;
And soon he was compelled to drop.
Sullivan's fists they fain had told
With marks severe on Morrissey bold,
Who said he yet his ground would hold
 At the fight at Boston Corners.
  Helter, skelter, &c., &c.

And thus they fought from round to round ;
Each closed with Yankee on the ground,
But 'twas considered hardly sound
 At the fight at Boston Corners.
Of rounds they ended thirty-six,
And Sullivan soon would Morrissey fix,
For the crowd all cried he's " good for nix"
But he said he'd show them some new 'tricks.'
And to make good the words he spoke,
He caught the Yankee round the throat,
And " bored" him fiercely on the rope
 At the fight at Boston Corners.
  Helter, skelter, &c., &c.

With rage the Yankee's face now burned,
But quick as thought he Morrissey turned,
And thus the money nearly earned,
 At the fight at Boston Corners.
Morrissey slipped down on his knee,
But this the Yankee did not see,
And sent his fist in rather free,
Which with the rules did not agree.
O'Donnell seeing the blow was " foul,"
At Sullivan rushed with a mighty howl,
And lent him one upon the jowl
 At the fight at Boston Corners.
  Helter, skelter, &c., &c.

The second of Yankee seeing the fun,
Up to O'Donnell quickly run,
And lent him one " clean as a gun,"
 At the fight at Boston Corners.
Morrissey jumped up off his knee,
And went straight to the referee,
And said " to time I'm here you see,
Of course you must decide for me."
The referee thinking all was right,
To Morrissey said you " win the fight."
While the latter quickly took his flight,
 From the ring at Boston Corners.
  Helter, skelter, &c , &c.

All this time the Yankee fought away,
With this one, that one, in his way,
Not thinking he had lost the day
 At the fight at Boston Corners.
The time-keeper wished to end the fun,
And said twas "time" the round begun,
But the people told him all was done,
And how the battle Morrissey won.
But Yankee called with all his might,
Upon his man to end the fight,
But Morrissey was out of sight,
 Of the ring at Boston Corners.
  Helter, skelter, &c., &c.

Lightning Source UK Ltd.
Milton Keynes UK
UKHW05n1037200718
325944UK00007BB/17/P